# Internal Auditing Guidebook

Steven M. Bragg

**Accounting**Tools®

Published by AccountingTools, Inc., Centennial, Colorado.

ISBN 978-1-64221-213-6

For more information about AccountingTools® products, visit our Web site at
www.accountingtools.com.

Printed in the United States of America

# Table of Contents

# About the Author

**Steven Bragg, CPA,** has been the chief financial officer or controller of four companies, as well as a consulting manager at Ernst & Young. He received a master's degree in finance from Bentley College, an MBA from Babson College, and a Bachelor's degree in Economics from the University of Maine. He has been a two-time president of the Colorado Mountain Club, and is an avid alpine skier, mountain biker, and certified master diver. Mr. Bragg resides in Centennial, Colorado. He has written more than 300 books and courses, including *New Controller Guidebook*, *GAAP Guidebook*, and *Payroll Management*.

Steven maintains the accountingtools.com web site, which contains continuing professional education courses, the Accounting Best Practices podcast, and thousands of articles on accounting subjects.

# Chapter 1
## Introduction to Internal Auditing

## Introduction

Internal audit refers to the department located within a business that monitors the efficacy of its processes and controls. The internal audit function is especially necessary in larger organizations with high levels of process complexity, where it is easier for process failures and control breaches to occur. The function is especially necessary in a publicly-held business, which must attest to the robustness of its systems of internal control. The internal audit function is quite valuable to these firms, because it provides them with the following value proposition:

- *Assurance services*. It provides the board of directors with assurance that the firm's governance, risk management, and system of controls are operating properly. This is an objective assessment of evidence to provide an opinion or a conclusion about the subject of the engagement.
- *Advisory services*. It provides in-house consulting services to enhance the efficiency and effectiveness of the firm, primarily through the examination of company processes and data. These engagements are typically performed at the specific request of the engagement customer.

A key point here is that the internal audit department is *not* responsible for the management of any governance practices, risk management activities, or control activities. Those responsibilities lie with the board of directors and the management team. Instead, the internal audit group sits apart from the rest of the company, evaluating and reporting on the effectiveness of these activities.

In addition, the department provides these services with complete objectivity, because it is committed to providing services with a high degree of integrity and accountability. Within this value proposition, the internal audit staff is responsible for the following activities:

- Fraud detection
- Information system assessments
- Internal control assessments
- Legal and regulatory compliance
- Operational efficiency assessments
- Process assessments
- Risk assessments
- Safeguarding of assets

Internal audit is not simply a watchdog that monitors a business and flags problems. It can also act as an internal consulting department that adds value to company operations. It does so by highlighting opportunities for improvement and facilitating changes within the organization. Given this broad mandate, an internal auditor can reasonably expect to engage in projects throughout an organization, including such areas as materials management, distribution, marketing, and production.

The internal audit department may be asked to provide information to virtually any stakeholder in a business, including its board of directors, managers, investors, regulators, and business partners. This is a much broader group than an external auditor deals with, which is usually limited to the hiring party (the audit committee).

## The Audit Committee

We just referred to the audit committee, which is responsible for overseeing the activities of the internal audit function. The committee is comprised of members of the board of directors, usually those with a reasonable degree of financial acumen. Depending on the situation, the committee has from three to five members, all of them being outside directors. It is an essential part of an organization's system of internal controls, because members of the board can have candid discussions with both the external and internal auditors without anyone from management being present. In order to properly oversee the internal audit department, it should follow these best practices:

Planning

- Evaluate the level of risk management coverage by the internal audit department. This is one of the essential oversight roles the board of directors, so the committee should have a significant interest in this area.
- Discuss the frequency of the department's planning updates. Ideally, the internal audit manager should be revising the departmental audit plan dynamically, as new issues arise within the company. It is usually considered inflexible to set the plan once a year and then rigidly adhere to it.

Services and Technology

- Assess the extent to which the internal audit staff is providing value to the organization. Besides the usual assurance services, internal auditors can provide data mining services and process flow suggestions to improve business unit performance.
- Examine the level of technology being used by the internal audit team. Ideally, they should be employing the latest data analysis tools to assist them in drawing conclusions from large data sets.

Personnel

- Ensure that there are regular meetings between the committee and the internal audit manager. Sponsoring regular presentations by the internal audit staff to the committee is a great way to build familiarity between the parties, as well as to educate committee members.
- Assess the extent to which the internal audit department is being used as a talent source for the rest of the company. Their broad knowledge of processes throughout the organization uniquely equips them for many possible roles.
- Oversee the training plan for the internal audit department. Staff members should be exposed to training in many areas, including data analysis, risk management, and governance processes. The training plan should be based on an analysis of the skills needed to be an effective department and the skills that its employees actually have.

## Assurance Services

As noted in the introduction, one of the key roles of the internal audit department is to provide assurance services, investigating whether the firm's governance, risk management, and system of controls are operating properly. More specifically, *governance* is the set of processes employed by the board to oversee how management fulfills the organization's objectives. *Risk management* is the set of processes used to identify and mitigate any uncertainties that may impact an organization. A *system of controls* is comprised of the policies and procedures used to ensure the integrity of a firm's financial information, promote accountability, and prevent fraud. The department assesses evidence relating to a targeted topic and generates conclusions from that analysis that are then shared with the board and management.

There are three parties involved in an assurance services arrangement. One is the *user*, who receives the auditor's report regarding the findings resulting from an engagement. Another party is the *auditor*, who conducts the work. The third party is the *auditee*, which is the party directly involved in the activity that is under review.

## Advisory Services

As noted in the introduction, the other key role of the department is to provide advisory services. These activities are usually requested by the *customer*, who is the party seeking assistance. This is typically a department manager, who wants the internal audit group to examine a particular issue impacting his or her area of responsibility, and provide advice on how to improve the situation.

## Special Public Company Services

The Sarbanes-Oxley Act imposes a particular burden on the chief executive officer (CEO) and chief financial officer (CFO) of any publicly-held company, which is to formally certify that the company's financial statements are accurate. The Act also requires that company management assess and report on the effectiveness of the company's internal control over financial reporting. These are significant responsibilities, since the Act imposes fines and jail time on those CEOs and CFOs whose financial statement certifications prove to be inaccurate. The best group within the organization that can assist the CEO and CFO with making these determinations is the internal audit department, since part of its job is the assessment of internal controls.

## Independence and Objectivity

Ideally, the internal audit department reports to the board of directors or the audit committee. By doing so, it remains independent of the management team, and so is able to investigate issues related to the team, reporting its findings back to the board. This level of independence means that the internal audit function cannot directly engage in company operations, since it would then be working for the management team it is supposed to be evaluating.

Objectivity is another key characteristic of the internal auditor. It involves having an unbiased impartial attitude toward one's work, so that no compromises are made in the development of work products. In order to be objective, the internal auditor cannot subordinate his or her judgment in regard to audit matters to other parties. In order to be objective, the internal auditor cannot become directly involved in day-to-day business operations or make any management decisions.

---

**EXAMPLE**

Jordan transfers into the internal audit department of a major consumer products company. He transferred in from the marketing department. In order to be objective about his work, the audit manager requires that he not be involved in any engagements involving the marketing department for a period of at least one year. Once a year has passed, it would be reasonable to expect that any work he had been involved with in the marketing department will no longer be subject to an internal audit review.

---

## Work Scheduling

The internal audit manager schedules audit work, usually focusing on high-risk areas. Other examinations may be conducted as directed by the audit committee, or as requested by department managers. The areas being targeted for an examination are normally given advance notice, so that they can assemble all required documents for the internal audit team. In some cases where fraud is suspected, the audit team will appear without any prior announcement, in hopes of catching the perpetrator.

The process followed for an engagement will vary somewhat, depending on the nature of the work. However, auditors will probably adhere to these steps:

1. *Obtain an understanding of the customer or auditee.* The auditor cannot provide relevant services without having a strong understanding of the customer or auditee, so a significant amount of time will be spent reviewing the relevant objectives, processes, risks, and business environment.

2. *Set engagement objectives*. The auditor begins with a specific set of objectives in order to develop a detailed work plan.
3. *Determine the evidence needed*. The auditor identifies the types of evidence needed in order to fulfill the objectives of the engagement.
4. *Define audit tests*. The auditor must decide upon the nature, timing, and extent of the audit tests that are needed to collect the evidence that was defined in the preceding step. There are many possible audit tests, such as inspecting documents and making inquiries, which will be covered in detail in a later chapter.
5. *Evaluate evidence*. The auditor needs to examine the results of the audit tests in order to reach conclusions. This can be an iterative process, where the initial results are unclear, and so require the use of additional tests.
6. *Communicate outcomes*. The auditor must assemble his or her findings into a clear statement of findings and recommendations, and communicate them to the user.

## The Differences Between Accounting and Internal Auditing

The accounting and internal audit departments are completely different departments, and are entirely disconnected. This is because the two departments are designed to perform different services for the organization. Here are several key differences:

- *Accounting transactions*. The accounting department records accounting transactions, while the internal audit department evaluates whether they were recorded correctly.
- *Data handling*. The accounting department aggregates massive amounts of financial data into the financial statements, while the internal audit department sorts through the same data, looking for irregularities or actionable recommendations.
- *Nature of the work*. The accounting department engages in constructive work, recording transactions and producing financial statements, while the internal audit department is analytical, investigating processes for errors.
- *Objective*. The accounting department's objective is to determine the financial results, financial position, and cash flows of the organization, while the internal audit department's objective is to add credibility to the financial statements and other reports of the company.
- *Processes*. The accounting department follows accounting policies and procedures in order to correctly record accounting transactions, while the internal audit department investigates whether the processes are functioning correctly and what changes to them may be needed.

# The Institute of Internal Auditors

The industry entity most commonly associated with support of the internal audit function is the Institute of Internal Auditors (IIA). The IIA engages in education, research, and advocacy on behalf of the internal audit profession. The Institute is a membership organization, founded in 1941, which offers the following general benefits to its members:

- Internal audit certification
- Internal audit training
- Job postings
- National conferences
- Networking with fellow Institute members
- Publications
- Research on internal auditing and related topics
- Webinars

The Institute conducts testing for the Certified Internal Auditor (CIA) designation, which is the primary certification awarded to internal auditors. After passing the examination, one must also complete a two-year internal auditing experience requirement before the certification will be awarded. Those awarded the CIA designation must maintain it by meeting continuing professional education requirements. The certification is useful for increasing the knowledge base of auditors, helping them gain credibility when applying for jobs, and enhancing their lifetime earnings potential.

The IIA has promulgated a set of core principles, a code of ethics, and a set of standards for the practice of internal auditing, which are summarized in the following sub-sections.

## Core Principles

The IIA developed a set of core principles that, when taken together, are intended to result in an effective internal audit function. These core principles are as follows:

- Demonstrates integrity
- Demonstrates competence and due professional care
- Is objective and free from undue influence
- Aligns with the strategies, objectives, and risks of the organization
- Is appropriately positioned and adequately resourced
- Demonstrates quality and continuous improvement
- Communicates effectively
- Provides risk-based assurance
- Is insightful, proactive, and future-focused
- Promotes organizational improvement

If an internal audit department falls short in any of these core principles, it implies that the group is not as effective in achieving its mission as it could be.

**Code of Ethics**

The IIA also promulgates a code of ethics, which states the principles and expectations associated with a person's behavior in the conduct of internal auditing. This code describes the minimum expected level of conduct, and points out expectations for specific types of behavior in certain circumstances. Its essential components are as follows:

Principles

- *Integrity.* A high level of integrity is needed to establish trust, which provides the basis for a user's reliance on the judgment of the internal auditor. Otherwise, a report recipient could not reasonably be expected to rely upon an internal auditor's report.
- *Objectivity.* An internal auditor is expected to exhibit the highest level of professional objectivity in collecting, reviewing, and communicating information about the activity or process under examination. One is expected to make a balanced assessment of relevant information, and not to be unduly influenced by one's own interests or others when forming judgments.
- *Confidentiality.* An internal auditor must respect the value and ownership of any information received, and so cannot disclose it without appropriate authorization to do so. There is an exception when there is a legal or professional obligation to disclose information.
- *Competency.* An internal auditor must be able to apply adequate knowledge, skills, and experience when conducting internal audit activities.

Rules of Conduct

- *Integrity.* An internal auditor shall perform work with honesty, diligence, and responsibility, observe the law, and not knowingly be part of any illegal activity or engage in acts that are discreditable to the profession. Further, the auditor shall respect the ethical objectives of the organization.
- *Objectivity.* An internal auditor shall not participate in any activity that could impair his or her unbiased assessment, including any activities that could conflict with the interests of the organization. This includes not accepting anything that could impair one's professional judgment. One should also disclose all material facts that, if not disclosed, could distort the reporting of any activities under review.
- *Confidentiality.* An internal auditor shall be prudent in the use of any information acquired in the course of his or her duties, and shall not use it for personal gain or in any way contrary to the law.
- *Competency.* An internal auditor shall only engage in services for which he or she has sufficient knowledge, skills, and experience, and shall strive to

continually improve their proficiency over time, as well as the effectiveness and quality of their work.

---

**EXAMPLE**

Doug accepts tickets to a local baseball game from the manager of a department in which Doug is investigating a possible case of fraud. The tickets include free parking and vouchers for free meals. This constitutes the acceptance of a gift from an auditee, which impairs his objectivity in regard to the audit work.

**EXAMPLE**

During an internal audit, Evan becomes aware of material nonpublic information regarding the company. Based on this information, he buys several thousand shares of company stock, which immediately appreciates in value once the information becomes known to the investment community. Evan has violated the confidentiality principle.

**EXAMPLE**

Sarah is an expert in derivatives accounting. She is asked to shift over from her position in the internal audit department to a temporary position in the accounting department to handle the derivatives accounting, until a full-time person can be found with the requisite experience. After this assignment is over, she should not perform any engagements related to derivatives accounting for at least a year, in order to avoid any risk of having an unbiased view of any results found.

---

When there is a breach of the IIA code of ethics, the IIA can only take action against the person if he or she is an IIA member or holds an IIA certification. In these cases, the IIA can elect to censure a member, or suspend or cancel the person's membership, along with the person's certification.

**Standards for the Practice of Internal Auditing**

The IIA publishes a set of standards for the professional practice of internal auditing. The purpose of these standards is as follows:

- To guide their adherence to those mandatory elements of the standards.
- To provide a framework for performing a number of internal auditing services.
- To provide a basis for the evaluation of their performance.
- To assist with the improvement of organizational processes and operations.

These standards and the preceding code of ethics constitute the mandatory elements of the IIA's International Professional Practices Framework.

The IIA's standards are divided into two categories, which are attribute standards and performance standards. Attribute standards cover the attributes of internal auditors and the organizations within which they work. These standards are divided into four sections, which are:

- 1000 series – Covers the topics of purpose, authority, and responsibility. The internal audit department must have a charter that states its purpose, authority, and specific responsibilities.

- 1100 series – Covers the topics of independence and objectivity. The internal audit department has to be independent, and have an unbiased attitude toward its work. These are essential requirements for the performance of assurance engagements, in particular.

- 1200 series – Covers the topics of proficiency and due professional care. Internal auditors must have a sufficiently high level of proficiency to competently complete the engagements to which they are assigned, or else their work output will be useless. They must also be reasonably prudent and competent in the conduct of their work.

- 1300 series – Covers the topics of quality assurance and improvement programs. A quality assurance program is needed within the internal audit department in order to install confidence by users and customers in the department's output. This program should be regularly evaluated, and the results communicated to senior management and the board of directors.

Performance standards address the nature of internal auditing and provide quality criteria for the measurement of auditor performance. Both categories of standards apply to all internal audit services. These standards are divided into seven sections, which are:

- 2000 series – Covers the management of all internal auditing activities. These standards delineate how the internal audit function can add value to the overall organization.
- 2100 series – Covers the nature of the internal auditing work to be performed. These standards show how to identify engagements that will enhance the organization, covering such areas as operational decisions, risk management, and the promotion of ethical values.
- 2200 series – Covers the planning of internal audit engagements. These standards address multiple planning considerations, setting objectives and engagement scope, allocating appropriate resources to the work, and developing an engagement work program.
- 2300 series – Covers the performance of internal audit engagements. These standards discuss the identification of information needed for an engagement, the need to analyze and evaluate it, and to document the findings.
- 2400 series – Covers the communication of engagement results. These standards describe the criteria for communicating engagement information to management and the board of directors, how to deal with errors and omissions, the proper dissemination of engagement results, and several related matters.

- 2500 series – Covers how engagement progress is to be monitored. This standard notes that a system is needed to periodically monitor the outcomes of any engagement results communicated to management.
- 2600 series – Covers how to communicate the acceptance of risks by management. This standard addresses what should be done when management has chosen to accept an unusually high risk level.

The attribute and performance standards are as follows:

Attribute Standards

**1000** – *Purpose, authority, and responsibility*. An internal audit charter should be used to define the purpose, authority, and responsibility of the internal audit function; it should be approved by the board of directors. This is needed to establish the department's position within the firm, as well as the scope of its activities. It should also authorize the department's access to records, personnel, and assets relating to the completion of audit engagements.

**1010** – *Recognizing mandatory guidance in the internal audit charter*. The internal audit charter should recognize that the IIA's core principles, code of ethics, and standards for the practice of internal auditing are mandatory. These items should be discussed with senior management and the board.

**1100** – *Independence and objectivity*. The internal audit department must be independent of the rest of the organization, and its staff must be objective in performing their assigned tasks.

**1110** – *Organizational independence*. The manager of the internal audit department must report to a party within the business that allows the department to fulfill its responsibilities. This independence must be confirmed with the board at least once a year. Ideally, this means that the manager reports directly to the board. If anyone attempts to interfere with internal audit activity, these attempts should be reported to the board.

**1111** – *Direct interaction with the board*. The manager of the internal audit department must communicate directly with the board.

**1112** – *Chief audit executive roles beyond internal auditing*. In cases where the manager of the internal audit department has responsibilities outside of the internal auditing arena, there must be safeguards in place to minimize any impairments to independence or objectivity. This could involve a periodic evaluation of the other responsibilities and reporting relationships.

**1120** – *Individual objectivity*. All internal auditors must possess an impartial, unbiased attitude, and also avoid any conflicts of interest. A conflict of interest can impair one's ability to perform his or her duties in an objective manner.

**1130** – *Impairment to independence or objectivity*. Disclosure to the appropriate parties is required if an auditor's independence or objectivity is impaired in fact or appearance. For example, one should refrain from assessing any operations for which one had been responsible within the past year. However, one may provide consulting services relating to operations for which the auditor had previously been responsible.

**1200** – *Proficiency and due professional care.* All internal auditors must perform engagements with proficiency and due professional care.

**1210** – *Proficiency.* All internal auditors must have the knowledge, skills, and other competencies needed to complete their individual responsibilities. Auditors may demonstrate their proficiency by obtaining relevant professional certifications and qualifications. One must have sufficient knowledge to evaluate the risk of fraud, as well as to evaluate key information technology risks and controls. Further, consulting engagements must be declined if the department does not have the competencies needed to perform the work.

**1220** – *Due professional care.* All internal auditors must exercise the care and skill expected of a reasonably prudent and competent internal auditor. This does not imply that the person is infallible. To meet this standard, one should consider the extent and complexity of the required work, the probability of significant errors, the cost-effectiveness of assurance activities, and several related matters.

**1230** – *Continuing professional development.* All internal auditors must enhance their skills and knowledge via ongoing professional development activities.

**1300** – *Quality assurance and improvement program.* The manager of the internal audit department must create and maintain a quality assurance and improvement program that addresses all aspects of the department's activities. This program enables one to evaluate conformance with the standards, and whether auditors are applying the IIA's code of ethics. Further, the program should assess the efficiency and effectiveness of the department's activities, and highlight areas that can be improved.

**1310** – *Requirements of the quality assurance and improvement program.* The aforementioned quality assurance and improvement program must include both internal and external assessments.

**1311** – *Internal assessments.* The aforementioned internal assessments must include ongoing internal audit monitoring and assessments within the organization by those with sufficient knowledge of the firm's internal audit activities.

**1312** – *External assessments.* A qualified, independent assessor must conduct an external assessment of the internal audit function at least once every five years. The form of this assessment, as well as the qualifications and independence of the assessor must be communicated to the board.

**1320** – *Reporting on the quality assurance and improvement program.* The results of the quality assurance and improvement program must be communicated to senior management and the board, noting the scope and frequency of these assessments, the conclusions reached, and any corrective action plans.

**1321** – *Use of "Conforms with the International Standards for the Professional Practice of Internal Auditing"*. Use of the statement "Conforms with the International Standards for the Professional Practice of Internal Auditing" is only appropriate when the internal audit program is supported by the results of a quality assurance and improvement program.

**1322** – *Disclosure of nonconformance*. Any nonconformance with the IIA's code of ethics or its standards must be disclosed to senior management and the Board, when this impacts the scope or operations of the internal audit function.

Performance Standards

**2000** – *Managing the internal audit activity*. The internal audit activity must be effectively managed to ensure that it adds value to the business. This happens when the department achieves the purpose stated in its charter, conforms to the IIA standards, considers emerging issues that could affect the organization, and its members conform to the IIA code of ethics.

**2010** – *Planning*. The internal audit department must have a risk-based plan to establish priorities, consistent with the goals of the firm. This includes adjusting the plan in response to any changes in the organization's operations, risks, processes, and controls.

**2020** – *Communication and approval*. The internal audit department's plans and resource requirements shall be communicated to senior management and the board for their approval. The impact of resource limitations must also be communicated to them.

**2030** – *Resource management*. The resources of the internal audit department must be appropriate, sufficient and properly deployed to achieve its approved plan. This primarily refers to having the proper knowledge and skills mix on staff.

**2040** – *Policies and procedures*. The internal audit department shall have policies and procedures to guide its activities. This depends on the size and structure of the department, as well as the complexity of the work it conducts.

**2050** – *Coordination and reliance*. The internal audit department shall share information and coordinate its activities with other service providers in order to ensure a proper level of coverage for the organization, and to lessen the duplication of effort.

**2060** – *Reporting to senior management and the board*. The internal audit manager must report to senior management and the board on a regular basis concerning the department's performance, as well as its conformance with the IIA's code of ethics and standards. This report should also include significant risk and control issues, as well as any other matters that require the attention of the recipients.

**2070** – *External service provider and organizational responsibility for internal auditing*. When internal auditing activities are being performed by an external service provider, it must make management and the board aware that the business is still responsible for maintaining an effective internal audit function. This is achieved with a quality assurance and improvement program.

**2100** – *Nature of work*. The internal audit department is tasked with evaluating and contributing the entity's governance, risk management, and control processes. The credibility of the department is enhanced when auditors are proactive about offering insights to assist the organization.

**2110** – *Governance*. The internal audit department should make improvement recommendations pertaining to strategic and operational decisions, risk management and control, and performance management. It should also promote proper ethics and values throughout the organization, as well as communicate risk and control information where needed within the firm.

**2120** – *Risk management*. The internal audit department must enhance risk management processes by evaluating their effectiveness. This is done by ensuring that risks are identified and assessed, and that reasonable risk responses are selected. There should also be a risk measurement system that feeds risk information to those responsible for it within the organization.

**2130** – *Control*. The internal audit department must evaluate the effectiveness and efficiency of the organization's controls by promoting ongoing improvements.

**2200** – *Engagement planning*. Internal auditors must develop a plan for each engagement, which includes the objectives, scope, and timing, as well as the resources needed. The plan should take into consideration the strategies and objectives of the organization, as well as any risks associated with the engagement.

**2201** – *Planning considerations*. Internal auditors should take the following items into consideration when planning an engagement:

- The strategies and objectives of the functional area being reviewed.
- The main risks to the function's objectives and operations, and how these risks can be mitigated.
- The adequacy of the function's governance, risk management, and control processes.
- The prospects for improving the function's governance, risk management, and control processes.

**2210** – *Engagement objectives*. Internal auditors must establish a set of objectives for each engagement, which is based on an assessment of relevant risks.

**2220** – *Engagement scope*. The scope of an engagement must be sufficiently broad to achieve the engagement objectives.

**2230** – *Engagement resource allocation*. Internal auditors must assign a sufficient amount of appropriate resources to achieve the engagement objectives. This is based on an evaluation of the nature and complexity of each engagement.

**2240** – *Engagement work program*. Internal auditors must develop work programs that are sufficient for achieving the engagement objectives. These programs should be approved prior to implementation.

**2300** – *Performing the engagement.* Internal auditors must identify, review, evaluate, and document a sufficient amount of information to achieve the objectives of each engagement.

**2310** – *Identifying information.* Internal auditors must identify a sufficient amount of reliable and relevant information to achieve the objectives of each engagement.

**2320** – *Analysis and evaluation.* Internal auditors must base their conclusions on appropriate analyses and evaluations.

**2330** – *Documenting information.* Internal auditors must develop documentation that is sufficient to support the conclusions reached. The department should have documentation custody and retention policies, including the circumstances under which it can be released to other parties.

**2340** – *Engagement supervision.* Internal audit engagements must be properly supervised, so that objectives are achieved, quality levels are assured, and the staff is properly developed. This will depend on the proficiency and experience of the internal audit staff, as well as the complexity of each engagement.

**2400** – *Communicating results.* The results of engagements must be properly communicated.

**2410** – *Criteria for communicating.* Communications relating to engagements must include their objectives, scope, and results (including conclusions and recommendations).

**2420** – *Quality of communications.* The communications made by internal auditors must be accurate, clear, objective, constructive, complete, and timely. This means that the communications should be free of errors or distortions, and representative of the underlying facts, as well as unbiased, easily understood, helpful to the organization, and include all significant and relevant information.

**2421** – *Errors and omissions.* If a communication contains a significant error or omission, corrected information should be sent to everyone who received the original communication.

**2430** – *Use of "Conducted in Conformance with the International Standards for the Professional Practice of Internal Auditing".* The internal audit department should only indicate that an engagement was conducted in conformity with the International Standards for the Professional Practice of Internal Auditing if the work is supported by the results of the department's quality assurance and improvement program.

**2431** – *Engagement disclosure of nonconformance.* When an engagement is impacted by nonconformance with the IIA's code of ethics or standards, any communication of the results of that engagement should include the nature of and reason for the nonconformance, as well as its impact on the engagement and its results.

**2440** – *Disseminating results.* The results of engagements must be communicated to the appropriate parties. The department manager is responsible for reviewing and approving these communications, and to whom the results will be communicated.

**2450** – *Overall opinions*. When the internal audit department issues an overall opinion, it must consider the strategies, objectives, and risks of the business, as well as the expectations of senior management and the board. The overall opinion must be based on sufficient, reliable, relevant, and useful information. The opinion should be accompanied by the scope of the engagement, a summary of supporting information, and the risk or control framework used to develop the opinion.

**2500** – *Monitoring progress*. A system must be established and maintained to monitor the disposition of any engagement results communicated to management.

**2600** – *Communicating the acceptance of risks*. When it appears that management has accepted a risk level that could be unacceptable to the organization, the internal audit manager must discuss the issue with senior management. If the matter cannot be resolved, then it should be communicated to the board. It is not the responsibility of the internal audit manager to resolve the identified risk.

## Internal Audit Career Path

Internal auditors most commonly enter the field from a public accounting firm. There are two reasons for this path; first, someone who has already gained practical experience as an auditor can slide into an internal auditing job relatively easily. And second, the individual is likely to be hired by a client, who has a chance to evaluate them over the course of an audit.

Another option is to be hired directly out of college, usually via a summer internship. These arrangements are more common when students have enrolled in an internal auditing program at college, so they already have a reasonable knowledge base from which to work. Their professors may recommend the more promising students to recruiters, which provides a seamless path into an internal audit position.

Yet another option is available in larger firms, whose human resources departments routinely rotate their more promising management candidates through the internal audit department. This is done in order to increase their knowledge of governance, risk management, and control issues across the entire organization.

A person does not normally stay in the internal audit department for his or her entire career. Instead, a more common path is to use the knowledge gained in this department to move up into a management position, either within the company or elsewhere. For those people who do choose to remain within the department, the most common option is to be promoted into the internal audit manager position, running the entire department. A third option is to be hired into a firm that provides internal auditing services to multiple clients, thereby allowing for advancement into a partner position.

In short, the internal auditor is considered to be a highly-skilled individual who can provide significant value to a business. Given that perception, it should be no surprise that internal auditors are viewed as being among the most likely people in a business to be promoted into more advanced positions.

## Summary

The internal audit function provides both assurance and consulting services to a business, under the oversight of the audit committee. In order to conduct its work properly, it needs to remain independent of the rest of the organization, so it cannot be directly responsible for any operating activities. The standards under which internal auditors work have been promulgated by the Institute of Internal Auditors, which also provides a certification program to auditors. In the following chapters, we delve further into the nature of the internal auditor's work, with a particular emphasis on assurance engagements.

# Chapter 2
# Governance

## Introduction

Any well-run organization that wants to make consistent and reliable decisions needs a framework for doing so. This is called a governance structure, and it is designed to provide direction to an organization's decision makers. The extent to which a governance structure is integrated into the organization dictates how well the needs of its stakeholders are met. The governance structure is also designed to set up boundaries regarding which actions are allowed and not allowed. The setting of boundaries allows a business to comply with all applicable laws and regulations, as well as its own code of ethics. Further, the governance structure provides guidelines for risk management. The structure should assist managers in making decisions about how to spot and manage any risks that could threaten the firm, and how to mitigate them. The structure can also provide direction about which risks the firm will accept in order to further its strategic direction. Finally, a system of controls is one of the most essential risk mitigation concepts in a business, and so represents an outcome of the governance structure. As we will discuss in this chapter, the internal audit department has a role to play in reviewing how well the governance structure operates within a business.

## The Governance Concept

Governance is a system of rules and processes by which an organization is directed and controlled. In essence, it involves working towards outcomes that balance the interests of the firm's stakeholders, such as its shareholders, business partners, lenders, creditors, regulatory agencies, and the community. These interests can be quite varied. For example, lenders and creditors expect to be paid on time, while regulators expect the company's products to meet certain safety standards, and shareholders expect to be paid a reasonable return on their investment. Some balancing of these interests will likely be needed, such as capping budgeted profits in order to invest in new pollution-reduction equipment for a factory. The general areas that will need to be addressed as part of this balancing discussion are as follows:

- *Compliance*. Considerations include balancing the cost of regulatory compliance against the cost of regulatory fines and restraining orders, as well as incurring costs to avoid the costs of litigation at a later date.
- *Financial*. Considerations include maintaining an adequate cash reserve to ensure liquidity, maintaining a sufficiently conservative capital structure to ensure a targeted credit rating, and generating enough profits (and dividends) to keep investors happy.
- *Operations*. Considerations include the cost to protect assets (such as with insurance), the cost to protect employees (with health and safety investments),

the cost to protect data (such as with encryption protocols), and ensuring that capacity constraints are closely monitored.

- *Strategy*. Considerations include making investments in the reputation of the business, and paying for targeted investments in growth opportunities for the firm.

---

**Note:** The minimum level of acceptable governance is to target a consistent, long-term level of profitability. However, it is becoming increasingly important for governance to address additional topics, such as having a low environmental impact and supporting the local community.

---

The board only sets governance guidelines and then delegates responsibility to management to enact them. Board members are not expected to delve into the details of day-to-day management of the enterprise. Instead, the guidelines they give management act as boundaries for what management is allowed to do, and within which managers can act relatively freely.

---

**EXAMPLE**

A board of directors sets boundaries for an auto parts retail business, stating that management is limited to opening stores within the United States, and that it cannot engage in car repair activities or in the distribution of new or used cars. Further, the board defines reporting thresholds for management, so that the board only has to be notified when individual store sales decline by more than 10%, when cash flows are projected to be insufficient to pay for the next dividend, and when overall profits decline by at least 5%.

---

One way in which management can ensure that the governance guidelines set by the board are followed is to establish a risk committee, which identifies all key risks, decides how to deal with them, and assigns responsibility for each one. As the organization changes, the risk committee re-evaluates how it is dealing with these key risks, while also identifying other risks that may apply to the new circumstances of the business. This committee is typically run by a member of senior management.

A reasonable concern for the board of directors is whether the management team is fulfilling the board's strategy, and whether it is doing so within the boundaries set by the board. In essence, it needs an independent reviewer function, which is an essential role of the internal audit department. In this role, auditors can review virtually any area of a business, though usually with a focus on high-risk areas, and report its findings back to the board. The board should have input into the work plans of the department, to ensure that auditors are engaged in tasks that provide assurances to the board that its governance structure is working (or not).

Though the internal audit department provides an essential assurance service for the board, this is not the only way to ensure that the governance structure is maintained properly. Under the *three lines of defense model*, a system of internal controls constitutes the first line of defense. Since controls are typically built directly into a company's procedures, they usually head off most issues that could impinge on the governance structure. However, controls are operated by people who are not independent of the areas being controlled, which constitutes a weakness. The second line of defense is comprised of a medley of assurance activities, such as the risk committee, a quality assurance group, and a health and safety group. These people are independent of those responsible for the system of controls, so they are much more likely to be independent and objective in making assessments. However, assurance is a part-time job for these people, which is why the third line of defense is needed – the internal audit department. Auditors are not responsible for any other activities, and their jobs are designed to be independent of the rest of the organization – which improves their ability to be objective when conducting engagements. When all three lines of defense are operating properly, it is much more likely that a firm's governance structure will operate as intended.

---

**Note:** Since governance provides a framework for attaining a firm's objectives, it spans most aspects of management, including budgets, internal controls, and measurement systems. This means that almost any management decision could be examined by internal auditors to see if it aligns with the firm's governance structure.

---

Governance refers to the strategic direction of the business and how the activities of the organization are monitored. Strategic direction is supported by a structure of objectives that are closely aligned with the priorities of stakeholders. This direction is intertwined with a specific level of risk-taking philosophy, as well as formal expectations for employee conduct.

---

**EXAMPLE**

Gulf Coast Insurance is in the business of providing property insurance to people living along the Gulf Coast of the United States. The governance structure that its board has put in place restricts its insurance coverage to this region, in order to focus its sales staff on a tightly-defined area. Since this area is subject to hurricanes, the board has also set up a risk management philosophy of never exceeding 5% of all property insurance policies in any county, so that a major hurricane event will not overwhelm the company's reserves. The board also mandates a fixed compensation structure for all salespeople, so that they do not have an incentive to over-sell insurance.

---

The oversight aspect of governance involves the use of policies, procedures, and controls that are specifically targeted at dictating behavior throughout an organization. This is where the internal audit department is most needed, for it must monitor how well those policies, procedures, and controls are driving the governance directives of the board. Whenever an internal auditing project spots a governance issue, the finding is passed to the management team for resolution, which may result in a policy, procedure, or control change. When the issue is a significant one, it may be brought before the board for its review.

---

**EXAMPLE**

An internal audit team at Mule Corporation, maker of the "Bad Ass" motorcycle, is investigating the quality practices of the firm's procurement department. Mule's board of directors has mandated that the company produce the highest-quality motorcycles in the world, both as a branding concept and to show its customers that it cares about their safety. The audit team finds that several purchasing managers have bought lower-quality shock absorbers, which could lead to catastrophic failures when the motorcycles are used on rougher terrain. This is a serious governance issue, since it breaches the Board's quality policy, as well as several purchasing procedures relating to management's review and approval of purchasing contracts.

---

## The Role of Internal Auditing

As just noted, the internal audit department serves as the third line of defense in maintaining a sufficient governance structure in a business. Besides conducting ongoing assurance activities and reporting their findings back to the board of directors, internal auditors can also provide the following services related to governance:

- Advise the board about emerging risk issues that may impact the organization.
- Aggregate and provide analysis on governance issues from around the company, and forward it to the board.
- Assist the board with its assessment of the external auditors it has retained to audit the company's financial statements.
- Assist the board with its performance self-assessment procedures.
- Provide a comparison of current board practices to what are considered best practices for board operations.
- Provide advice about the company's escalation policy for bringing matters to the attention of the board.
- Provide advice about the proper role, authorizations, and responsibilities of the audit committee.
- Provide information to the audit committee as needed for its oversight of the internal audit department.

## Summary

An effective governance structure is one of the core underlying issues contributing to the success of a business. The internal audit department should be routinely involved in an examination of every component of the governance structure, including internal controls, risk management, and how well the organization is complying with that structure. This should be a continual feedback loop, where the auditors routinely provide their findings to the board of directors, which then adjusts the governance structure as needed.

# Chapter 3
# Risk Management

## Introduction

Risk equates to uncertainty regarding a future outcome. A business is filled with uncertainty, for there are few situations in which the outcome can be predicted with complete reliability. For example, a business has several thousand outstanding accounts receivable – exactly how many of them will become bad debts? Similarly, a business requires a key commodity as a raw material in the construction of a product – can it predict exactly what the price of this commodity will be in one year? Or, it will cost $250 million to develop a new drug and have it approved – but how certain is the approval? In these cases, it is impossible to predict the exact outcome.

Uncertainty is pervasive, and yet managers routinely ignore the concept of variable outcomes. Instead, they use budgets to derive a single view of the future, and are then perturbed when they cannot force their organizations to deliver results that precisely match the outcome predicted in the budget. This is because there may be thousands of uncertain events that all impact the financial results of a business. Despite management's best efforts, it is nearly impossible to deliver actual results that match the original budgeted prediction.

A better way to see the impact of risk is to view an organization as a portfolio of risks, each of which is derived from any number of management decisions made in the past. Some decisions, such as expanding an existing product line, are more likely to result in modest profits or losses. Other decisions, such as the funding of a portable fusion reactor product, could be spectacularly successful or drive a firm into bankruptcy. Some may produce offsetting gains and losses, resulting in modest net changes. One should be cognizant of the more crucial of these risks, sometimes to take advantage of them and at other times to reduce them.

In this chapter, we describe the concept of risk management, how to incorporate it into an organization's overall strategy, who is responsible for it, the role of the internal audit department, and several related matters.

## Benefits of Risk Management

There are a number of reasons why an organization should manage its risks. The central issues are the ability to smooth out earnings or to enhance earnings.

Risk management can be used to mitigate the occurrence of unusual expenses, so that the actual expenses incurred are much closer to budgeted expectations. This is particularly important for a publicly held company, which can then give the investment community reliable guidance about its future results. When a business consistently reports earnings that do not vary much from predictions, investors will probably keep the stock price within a relatively narrow range, and there will be no reason for any investors to engage in short selling. Another benefit is that reliable earnings attract lenders, so that a business is more likely to be offered reasonable interest rates and longer-term lending arrangements. Lower interest rates reduce the cost of a firm's capital, so that it can invest in more projects that have lower projected returns. Having longer-term debt arrangements means that a business can more easily weather market crises, since it does not have to constantly roll over its debt into new loans.

One can enhance earnings by actively identifying opportunities that are risky, but which also generate high returns. For example, an organization might choose to start doing business in a country where profits could be substantial, but where there is also a risk of a currency devaluation. Taking this approach can result in higher profits, but those profits are also likely to be more variable – very high in some periods, but with notable losses in others. This use of risk management works well when the management team is willing to aggressively pursue profits.

The most likely scenario in a well-managed business is that management takes advantage of both types of risk management. They are well aware of the risks to which the business is subjected, and take steps to mitigate risks in certain areas while accepting the risk associated with selected business opportunities.

The amount of risk taken on by a business depends on the comfort level of the management team. Some may prefer a highly stable environment from which the probability of risk has largely been reduced, while others are more comfortable taking large chances throughout the organization in order to pursue the possibility of maximizing profits.

## The Interrelationship between Risk and Strategy

The two preceding benefits of risk management can be incorporated into an entity's strategic planning. When the management team considers the strategic direction of a business, a major part of the analysis should center on the risks that are linked to each possible strategic alternative, and how to handle those risks. Since there may be a number of strategic alternatives with many risks attached to each one, the planners will need to focus on just the most critical risks associated with each strategy, and develop the following information:

- The likelihood of occurrence
- The cost per occurrence
- Mitigation alternatives

Ideally, each proposed strategy should outline key risks, how risks are to be mitigated or off-loaded, *or* the cost of retaining the risks. The senior management team can then review this risk summary as part of its analysis of strategic alternatives.

### Risk Retention Strategy

Not all risks can be successfully mitigated. Some types of risk can be expensive to guard against, perhaps with relatively expensive hedging contracts. Consequently, there should be some level of risk that it is more economical over the long-term for a business to retain.

The amount of risk that a business is willing to retain is strongly influenced by its financial position. For example, a company with significant market share, profitability, and cash reserves can easily withstand the financial losses associated with risk. Conversely, a company that is highly leveraged and which uses much of its cash to pay off loan principal can afford to retain very little risk.

This ability to retain risk can have a profound impact on the overall strategy of a business. In essence, a financially stable entity is in a much better position to dabble in new lines of business that offer major upside potential, but which also run the risk of significant losses.

---

**EXAMPLE**

The management team of the thermometer manufacturer Kelvin Corporation has just completed a leveraged buyout of the founder, which involves taking on $10 million of high-cost debt that must be paid off within the next five years. For this period, the sole focus of the management team is on paying off the debt. The company cannot afford to risk any funds on new product development.

At the same time, Celsius Corporation has just raised money through a major new stock offering, and is risking $5 million on the development of a new lineup of remote temperature sensors that use the theory of quantum entanglement to track temperature readings from thousands of miles away. There is a significant risk that the development project will fail, but the upside potential is complete patent protection in a large new market.

Given the financial circumstances of the two companies, Kelvin cannot afford to take on any risk, while the management of Celsius has so much money that it can take on highly risky projects.

---

## Risk Analysis as an Opportunity

The analysis of potential risk to which a business is subjected should not be a casual affair, but rather a studied one. This means keeping a running list of problems that other companies have encountered within the industry and in adjacent industries, and reviewing the list at regular intervals to see if events have made any risks more or less likely. The internal audit department can take on a consulting role in providing this information.

The identification of risks may present opportunities; a company could launch initiatives in new areas that competitors might consider excessively risky. This is particularly likely when a higher level of risk is accompanied by a greater chance of reward.

**EXAMPLE**

There is a general dearth of storefronts near a certain section of coastline, since it has been hit by three hurricanes in the past ten years. A real estate company is fully aware of the hurricane risk, and develops a new building design that mitigates the risk of storm damage by elevating the first floor of the building, leaving room for storm waters to flow under the building. The company successfully builds and operates these structures, which survive several additional hurricanes with minimal damage. In this case, the company is fully aware of the risks, and chooses to proceed in a manner that mitigates those risks.

**EXAMPLE**

A CPA firm has just been devastated by a major tornado that wiped out a large part of the city in which it is located. It could take the prudent path of following the other CPA firms out of town, to relocate to a safer city. Instead, the partners decide to construct a robust safe room for the employees that will also contain client files, and markets this upgrade as a document storage facility for clients. The result is a major boost in business, especially since most of the other CPA firms have fled the city.

A reverse way of looking at risk-related opportunities is to evaluate when to exit an excessively staid business. A low-risk environment tends to also generate low returns, so it can make sense to see if any product lines or customers that have a combination of low risk and low reward should be eliminated.

**EXAMPLE**

Gulf Coast Insurance is evaluating its hurricane insurance to see if there are any opportunities to improve its overall rate of return. An examination by geographic region discovers that the Tallahassee area has not borne the brunt of a hurricane for some time, which has resulted in a gradual decline in the insurance rates that can be competitively set in this area. Management concludes that the margins are too low in this region, so it elects not to renew policies in this area, and instead focuses its sales force on other areas where the claim risk is higher, but where prices are also higher.

## Special Risk Situations

A business is at its most vulnerable when it is just beginning, since there is likely to be very little capital invested. In this state, even a minor perturbation in the business model could cause the entity to collapse. The situation is worsened by the management team's lack of knowledge of their business environment. They are probably figuring out how their chosen niche works as they develop the business, and so are surrounded by uncertainty.

In this situation, it is absolutely necessary to be aware of the risks to which the business is subjected, and mitigate them to the greatest extent possible. Given the minimal amount of capital available that can be used to absorb losses, the management team cannot afford to leave any significant risk unaddressed.

An organization may find great success if it concentrates its efforts into a small niche area. By doing so, it can build great expertise and tightly focused products that competitors cannot match. However, this success comes at a price, for it may also mean that there are only a small number of potential customers. If so, the firm might find that it is granting large amounts of credit to a small number of customers. If one of these customers cannot pay on time (or at all), the business could be in serious financial trouble.

This situation illustrates an inherent risk of concentrating too tightly on a market niche. To reduce the risk, it may be necessary to expand an organization's business somewhat to encompass an adjacent niche that will increase the number of customers.

## Risk Management for the Enterprise

We have just established that the management team should be highly cognizant of the risks to which their organization is subjected. How is this risk to be managed? At the lowest level of effectiveness, those managers who accept the concept of risk will monitor and act on it within their departments. However, this is not especially effective, since some departments are not addressing risk at all, and there is no consistency in the measurements and actions taken even in those situations where department managers are actively pursuing risk management. Worse yet, there is no recognition of risks that occur across multiple departments. In these cases, a risk may appear to be minimal when considered separately in several departments, and yet is a serious concern when viewed in aggregate. These issues lead us to the conclusion that the only way to effectively deal with risk is in a coordinated manner, across the entire enterprise. This concept is called *enterprise risk management*, or ERM.

An ERM system provides a consistent methodology for locating, measuring, and reporting on risks throughout an organization. It is also used to consider the impact of macroeconomic effects on an entire business, such as changes in interest rates, commodity prices, and inflation rates on the business as a whole. Further, the system provides for a central coordinating authority in the person of a chief risk officer (CRO). The CRO position is described in the next section.

ERM considers the effects of risk across an entire enterprise. When risk is mitigated at the local level, it is entirely possible that derivatives and insurance will be used in excessive amounts, which would be reduced if local managers were aware of countervailing transactions elsewhere in the business. For example, one business unit might be liable for a payment of $100,000 Canadian dollars in three months, and so plans to hedge the transaction. However, a different unit might expect to receive an $80,000 payment in Canadian dollars at the same time (which it plans to hedge), so the net amount at risk is only $20,000 Canadian dollars. From the perspective of the local business units, the company will be paying for hedges of $180,000 Canadian dollars, whereas from an ERM perspective, it would be apparent that the amount to be hedged should be only $20,000 Canadian dollars. Thus, ERM is useful for identifying residual risk, which can be much less expensive to deal with.

## The Chief Risk Officer

The chief risk officer (CRO) of a business is considered a mid-level to senior-level manager. This individual may work alone in a smaller organization, or have a staff in a larger, multi-location enterprise. The CRO oversees the following activities:

- Create an integrated risk framework for the entire organization
- Assess risk throughout the organization
- Quantify risk limits
- Develop plans to mitigate risks
- Advise on directing capital to projects based on risk
- Assist functional managers in obtaining risk mitigation funding
- Monitor the progress of risk mitigation activities
- Create and disseminate risk measurements and reports
- Communicate to key stakeholders regarding the risk profile of the business

The CRO may be assigned a number of additional tasks besides the main ones already noted. They include:

- *Oversee insurance.* Decide upon the types and specifics of the various insurance policies that the organization should buy. This includes being the contact person for the insurance providers.
- *Recommend insurance alternatives.* Recommend any alternative insurance features that are not currently being used, or suggest using insurance products that are entirely new to the company.
- *Manage claims.* Supervise the filing of insurance claims, monitor their progress with insurers, and verify that payments have been received.
- *Conduct due diligence.* Investigate the risks inherent in a target company that may be acquired, as well as the state of its risk management practices.

None of the preceding activities place direct responsibility for risk mitigation on the CRO. Instead, the CRO is considered to be an advisory position that brings risk issues to the attention of the rest of the organization. Since the CRO position is essentially an advisory one, this individual needs strong support from the chief executive officer (CEO), or is at risk of being ignored by the other managers. Consequently, the CEO needs to publicly voice his or her support of risk management, while also integrating an emphasis on risk management into the company's reporting structure and performance management system. The CEO's efforts will have succeeded when risk issues are naturally included in the daily discussion of operations amongst the management team.

A key concern when determining a reporting relationship for the CRO is that the senior management team may itself be causing a business to take on an unacceptable amount of risk. For example, if the CEO is determined to triple sales, this may require the business to sell to much riskier customers. Given this possibility, the CRO could be rendered ineffective by reporting to anyone in the management group. Under this scenario, it could make sense to have the CRO report either directly to the board of directors or a committee of the board.

## Risk Management Committee

The CRO chairs a risk management committee, which must make final determinations regarding whether risks should be mitigated or accepted. If risks are to be mitigated, the committee must also decide how this is to be done (such as buying insurance). Given the ramifications of these decisions, the members of the committee should be drawn from the senior management team. These decisions cannot be forced down further into the organization, given the potential size of the financial and operational ramifications.

If the risk management committee is sufficiently broad-based, it can also be used as a general support mechanism for risk management throughout a business. For example, if the heads of all major departments are members of the committee, it is much easier for this group to enforce a general sense of risk awareness among their subordinates.

Given the preceding point about the need for broad participation in the committee, the following individuals are commonly included in the committee:

- *Chief operating officer*. This person is at least responsible for production and materials management, which covers supply chain risks and a number of internal risk issues.
- *Chief financial officer*. This person is responsible for both treasury and accounting, where many financial risks arise, and so is among the most critical members.
- *Vice president of sales*. This person is responsible for relations with customers, and so must be aware of risk issues arising from that direction.
- *Vice president of strategic planning*. The development of strategic plans requires a detailed knowledge of the risks that arise from each possible strategic direction to be taken or avoided.
- *Vice president of human resources*. Many types of risks are associated with the hiring, treatment, and deployment of personnel, for which this person is either directly responsible or has an advisory role.
- *Internal audit manager*. This person is deeply involved in the corporate system of controls and ongoing testing of it, and so has a daily involvement with systems-related risks.

Finally, the chief executive officer should certainly be a member of the committee, since the risk outcomes of a business can have a profound impact on its financial results and ability to stay in business.

## Responsibility for Risk

We have already pointed out that the CRO is really present to place an emphasis on risk within a business, but is not actually responsible for it – indeed, the position does not have sufficient authority to have ultimate responsibility. The trouble is that risk is so pervasive within an organization that no one individual can solely generate an effective and company-wide approach to risk mitigation. Instead, a number of people must be involved. These individuals include:

1. *Functional managers.* Ultimately, those in the best position to enact risk mitigation tactics are those managers directly responsible for functional areas, such as the managers of the treasury, production, and sales departments. These individuals already have direct control over their areas of responsibility, and so can readily add risk management to their portfolios.

2. *Advisors.* The functional managers may not have enough expertise to deal with risk issues by themselves, and so may need to call in specialists to advise them on the best actions to take. For example, a consultant may be hired to advise on the legal aspects of environmental remediation liabilities, or an insurance advisor is called in to discuss the standard exclusions from flood insurance. The internal audit department can also provide consulting services.

3. *Chief risk officer.* The CRO coordinates the general risk management effort, which may include bringing in advisors for the functional managers. However, the CRO is removed somewhat from actually taking action regarding risk, and so is third in this priority listing.

4. *Chief executive officer.* The CEO is ultimately responsible for all actions taken, and so has a strong incentive to authorize significant actions to deal with risk. Nonetheless, this person is well away from the actual management of risk, and so is listed fourth in priority for risk management.

5. *Board of directors.* This group may have a risk committee, and may directly supervise the CRO. In addition, the board sets the tone throughout the organization for how risk is to be dealt with, by way of its governance framework. For the board to be effective in this area, it should be well-trained in risk management concepts, meet frequently enough to stay abreast of risk issues, and routinely question management about how it is dealing with risk. It is also helpful if the board members come from outside the organization and have no financial ties to it, since they can then be more objective in examining how the firm is managed.

The individuals noted in the preceding list are much more likely to take action regarding a risk situation if they hear about the problem. Ensuring that the responsible parties are notified of issues is a real concern, since information about problems tends to remain in the lower levels of many organizations. This issue can be counteracted by constantly communicating the need to push this information up to senior management. Also, it helps to have a flat corporate hierarchy, where there are fewer levels of management between front-line workers and senior management. The internal audit department can assist by evaluating how well risk reporting is being conducted throughout the organization.

## The Role of Internal Auditing

The internal audit department addresses risk management by evaluating the effectiveness of existing risk management processes and recommending improvements to them. This includes ongoing evaluations of how well company operations function, the firm's compliance with the law, and whether risk issues are being fully reported to senior management and the board in a timely manner. More specifically, internal auditors could reasonably expect to engage in the following activities:

- Evaluate how well risks are being managed.
- Evaluate how well risk management processes are functioning.
- Evaluate how well risks are being reported to senior management and the board.
- Assist in the identification and evaluation of risk, with an emphasis on risks that are not currently being considered.
- Advise management on how to respond to risks, including the advisability of those responses already chosen by management.
- Participate in the development of a risk management strategy for the organization.

Conversely, they should not take a direct role in the management of risk, since doing so interferes with their independence. This means staying away from any decisions on risk responses, or implementing risk responses. This means that the internal audit manager should not be directly accountable for risk management in any way. Instead, internal auditors should be limited to assurance and consulting activities.

The exact nature of the department in the risk management process will depend upon the abilities of the internal audit team.

> **Tip:** To keep internal auditors from being held responsible for risk management, ensure that this issue is specifically addressed in the department's charter.

## Types of Risks

Any company is subject to a large number of risks. To better understand them, it is useful to classify them into different categories. By doing so, one can adopt category-specific tactics to mitigate or transfer risk. Common risk categories are:

*Business risk* – The organization does not generate sufficient financial results to satisfy its owners. For example:

- A business reports unusually low earnings per share, resulting in the sale of its shares by many investors, which lowers the share price substantially.
- A retailer reports a decline in same-store sales, after which investors vote for a change in the board of directors, which in turn fires the entire management team.

*Compliance risk* – The organization violates the law, and incurs penalties as a result. For example:

- An airline suffers from several plane crashes. A government probe finds that the airline was skimping on its maintenance procedures, and forcibly shuts down the business.
- An oil drilling company suffers a major underwater drilling failure, resulting in a million-barrel oil spill into the ocean. The affected government immediately sues the company for several billion dollars.

*Credit risk* – The organization's customers, suppliers, or counterparties to other transactions do not meet their obligations to the business. For example:

- A major customer goes bankrupt, leaving the seller with a massive bad debt that likely cannot be recovered.
- A supplier takes a large advance payment for a custom order and then goes bankrupt, leaving the buyer with little prospect for a recovery.
- A supplier is only able to ship part of an order to the buyer, because it does not have sufficient cash to buy the raw materials needed to complete the order, resulting in disruptions in the buyer's operations.

*Liquidity risk* – The organization does not have sufficient cash to meet its obligations. For example:

- A company grows so fast that its working capital requirements soak up all available cash. As a result, the business cannot pay its employees, so a competitor scoops up the firm during bankruptcy proceedings.
- The credit market unexpectedly tightens, so that a company cannot renew its line of credit or find an alternative lender.
- A company's credit rating is unexpectedly downgraded, making it much more difficult to sell bonds to investors.

*Market risk* – The market prices of goods and services, loans and investments, and other financial instruments that an organization depends on move in an unfavorable direction. For example:

- A company takes on a large amount of short-term debt in order to fund a production line expansion. Interest rates then increase, and the company finds that its new venture does not return enough cash to pay the higher interest rate.
- A company buys expensive equipment from a foreign supplier. By the time the invoice is due for payment, the relevant foreign exchange rate has moved sharply in an unfavorable direction, resulting in a much larger amount for the company to pay.

- A business buys petroleum products in bulk and converts them into plastic goods. Its input prices can vary substantially, while it is constrained from passing price increases through to its customers.

*Operating risk* – The organization suffers losses from failures by its employees, processes, or systems. Acts of nature fall into this category. For example:

- A treasury employee manages to transfer several million dollars of company money to his private account in Grand Cayman.
- Flooding in Thailand destroys a factory that a business was depending on for the electronic components used in its products.
- A bank's computer system crashes, wiping out the records of its depositors and borrowers.

The most dangerous type of risk is *strategic risk*, which interferes with a company's business model. A strategic risk undermines the value proposition which attracts customers and generates profits. For example, if a company's business model is to be the low-cost provider of a product and a competitor from a low-wage country suddenly enters the market, the company will find that its value proposition has been destroyed. Examples of strategic risk scenarios are:

- A new product fails catastrophically
- A major acquisition fails
- A customer gains massive market share and then has an inordinate ability to set prices
- A supplier gains monopoly control over supplies and raises raw material prices
- A key product goes off patent
- There is a sudden shift in technology that makes the company's products obsolete
- The contamination of company products with a hazardous substance leads to brand erosion
- The government changes its tax policy, which eliminates a key pricing advantage built into a firm's business model
- A trade agreement reduces barriers to entry, resulting in a flood of new competitors into the market
- Company assets are nationalized
- Terrorist attacks reduce sales or destroy property

The types of risks to which a business is subjected will vary considerably by company, since risk is based on such factors as geography, industry, product type, and employee relations. Thus, the risk mix is unique to every business. For example, a mining company is subject to the risk of a local shutdown by people who object to local pollution issues, while a business in the apparel industry may face a customer revolt over the working conditions of employees at its foreign clothing factories.

## Special Risk Situations

The preceding risk profile is a good way to slot a large number of potential risks into readily identifiable classifications. But what if a number of correlated risks occur at the same time? These "perfect storm" events are quite rare, but *do* happen. The key issue with perfect storm events is that they do not easily fit within a single classification. Instead, there tends to be a general triggering of multiple risks across several classifications that have a major negative impact on an organization – and the trigger is an unanticipated event. For example, a large earthquake hits Haiti, which triggers a tsunami that destroys shore properties all over the Caribbean. An operator of tourist resorts with multiple properties across the Caribbean could be nearly destroyed by such an event. Or, a clothing retailer's five key suppliers are all located in Bangladesh, which suffers catastrophic flooding as part of the annual monsoon season, thereby shutting down all deliveries to the retailer for months.

It can be exceedingly difficult to anticipate perfect storm events, because they are so rare, and may be triggered by events far away from the organization. Nonetheless, there are several ways to spot potential perfect storms, which are:

- *Geographical view.* Create a geographical model of where all company facilities and the facilities of its suppliers and customers are located. Then layer onto this model the natural disasters that can occur in each of these areas, and along the supply lines between the various facilities. This can trigger discussions of possible perfect storm events.
- *Correlation view.* Work through the risk categories listed earlier, and consider the types of triggering events that could impact multiple categories of risk, either at once or in a cascading manner.
- *Historical view.* Work back through a history of the industry for many years to determine what types of events have occurred in the past, no matter how infrequently, and see if any of them could apply to the company's current circumstances, perhaps in a modified form.

Risks may be ignored or incorrectly considered to have reduced effects when they are spread across or shared with several functional areas of a business. In this situation, the following issues can arise:

- When a risk applies to two or more functional areas, there can be a tendency for the manager of each function to assume that the other manager is responsible for it, so that no risk mitigation activities occur.
- A risk that is considered moderate or minor for one area may be present for several areas; if the risk occurs, it then impacts a broad swathe of the company's functionality, and is more likely to be classified as a major risk.

Both of these issues can be addressed through a heightened level of coordination across the functional areas, which means that risk mitigation requires the cooperation of all company departments.

## The Risk Management Process Flow

There should be a consistent process for identifying, quantifying, and dealing with risk. A more scattershot approach is likely to result in significant risks never being addressed. The general flow to follow is:

1. *Identify risks*. This can involve employee surveys or questionnaires, and/or the use of consultants who have a deep knowledge of the industry. If the management team has many years of experience in the industry, it might limit itself to using internal meetings to derive risks, without polling employees outside of this group. It is useful to view an organization from many perspectives to extract all possible risks. For example:

   - *Internal capacity*. Are the various functional areas of the company able to handle increased sales or other types of transactions? For example, what would happen to the accounting department's ability to operate if management were to engage in a minimum of three acquisitions per year?
   - *Inherent internal risks*. Are there risks that "come with the territory" in certain departments; these risks cannot be sidestepped or mitigated. For example, there is a high risk of losing IT personnel, due to shortages in the market for their skills.
   - *Impact of supply chain*. What would be the impact on the business if a major supplier or the supplier of a strategic part were unable to make deliveries? For example, a supplier might be purchased by a competitor, which intends to reserve all of the supplier's output for itself.
   - *Impact of customers*. Is the business able to support additional customers? For example, how would the organization deal with the demands of a large retail chain? There may not be sufficient customer service personnel, and returns may increase by several orders of magnitude.
   - *Future trends*. Are there discernible trends that can alter risks? For example, will the increased amount of social media usage increase the number of poor on-line reviews for a business?
   - *Historical risks*. Comb through the industry records to see if certain risks have appeared, even if only a few times or just once. The circumstances may change enough for these issues to appear again, though perhaps in a modified form.
   - *Competitor risks*. Are competitors noting any unusual risks in their financial reports or investor communications? If so, these risks may soon trouble a company's own operations.

   These risks can be summarized into a risk profile, which is described later in the Risk Profile sub-section.
2. *Rank risks*. There may be hundreds of possible risks that could impact an organization, so they must be prioritized to focus attention on the key items.

This is typically based on their frequency and severity, which can be plotted on a grid that uses frequency and severity as the axes. Severity can be measured by conducting a what-if analysis that reveals the full impact of a risk event on a business. The outcome should show the extent of losses and any reduction of cash reserves.

3. *Mitigate risks.* There are a variety of internal actions that can be taken to mitigate risk, such as moving a factory away from a flood plain or selling off a subsidiary that might otherwise be nationalized. Or, if there is a risk of product failure in the marketplace, consider developing two products at the same time. As another example, the risk of expropriation can be dealt with by halting the investment in the at-risk country or even selling off facilities in that country.

4. *Accept risks.* The likely payout from a risk may be so small that the company can easily bear the risk of loss. Alternatively, the offsetting amount of profit may be so high that the company is willing to accept a substantial amount of risk. For example, there could be a potential for massive profits from a new technology, though the development process could fail.

5. *Transfer risk.* If management cannot mitigate a risk and is unwilling to accept it, the remaining option is to transfer it to another party, usually an insurer.

6. *Report on the status of risks.* The management team must know if risks are changing, especially in a more frequent or more severe direction. Accordingly, there should be a reporting system in place that focuses attention on key risk "movers," without bogging down the reporting with other risks whose status is unchanged. In addition, a decision must be made about the frequency of reporting. Excessively frequent reporting may be ignored, while reports issued at long intervals may allow new risks to fester without proper management attention.

7. *Repeat.* Repeat the process at regular intervals and especially when there are major changes in a business that might strip away existing risks or introduce new ones, such as entry into a new market or the launch of a new product line. The iterative nature of the risk management process flow cannot be overemphasized, since an organization can learn from its actions in previous iterations to arrive at better risk management solutions in the future. The internal audit department should routinely assess how well this process works, and report its findings to senior management and the board.

## Risk Rankings

The ranking of risks can be difficult, for they cannot always be quantified. For example, the risk of a product recall can probably be quantified in terms of a range of product repair costs, but cannot be quantified in terms of the damage to the brand. The first figure could be reliably stated as falling somewhere between $800,000 and $1,000,000, but the cost of brand damage could extend for years and involve many lost customers who will no longer automatically turn to the company for replacement products. Consequently, an analysis of the frequency and severity of risks will require a significant amount of judgment, rather than hard numerical analysis. This hardly means that a ranking system should be ignored – judgment can be based on many years of experience, and may result in risk rankings that prove to be fairly accurate.

Given the difficulty of quantification, it can be difficult to assemble an exact ranking of which specific risks are more critical than others. Instead, it can make more sense to use a simple scale to measure a risk's frequency and severity, and concentrate attention on the cluster of risks that score the highest. We illustrate this concept in the following chart, which uses a zero-to-five scale to rate each risk.

Note in the sample table that there is a clear differentiation between three key risks (supplier damage, delivery disruptions, and bottleneck issues) and the remaining risk topics, which would certainly direct management's attention toward these items. At a lesser degree of risk, the chart shows a high frequency for commodity price swings, as well as high severity levels for hurricanes at one location and the risk of a pollution-related shutdown. The remaining risks are a combination of low severity and low frequency, and so would likely receive less management attention.

## Sample Risk Rankings Chart

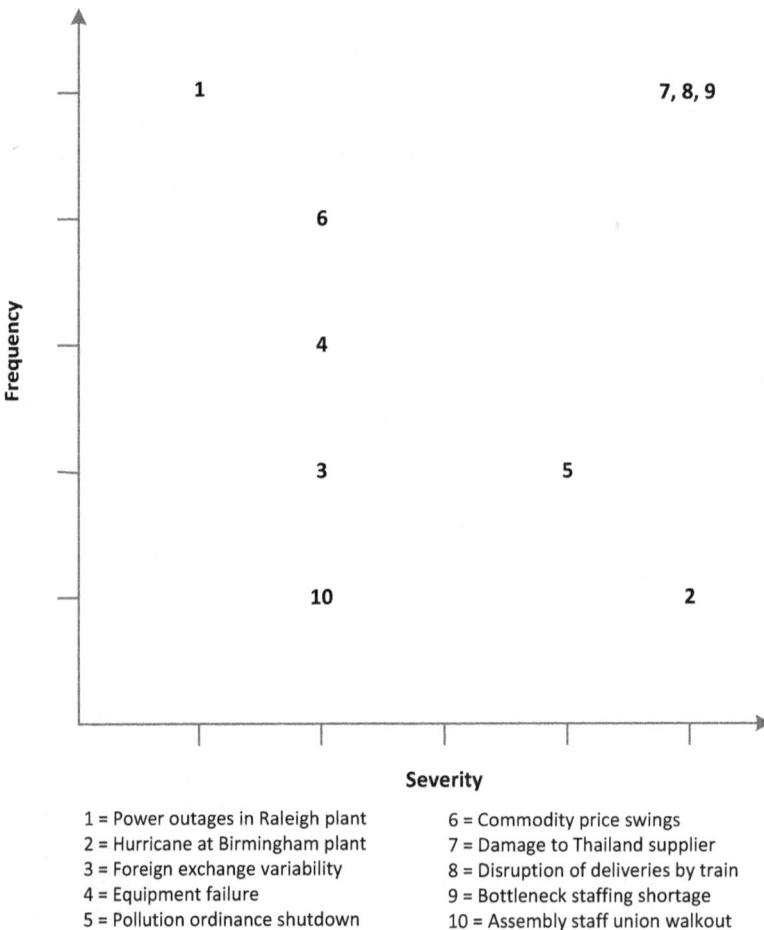

| | |
|---|---|
| 1 = Power outages in Raleigh plant | 6 = Commodity price swings |
| 2 = Hurricane at Birmingham plant | 7 = Damage to Thailand supplier |
| 3 = Foreign exchange variability | 8 = Disruption of deliveries by train |
| 4 = Equipment failure | 9 = Bottleneck staffing shortage |
| 5 = Pollution ordinance shutdown | 10 = Assembly staff union walkout |

The zero-to-five scale used in the sample chart can be clarified in greater detail, so that those people deriving scores for risks can set scores with a fair degree of reliability. For example, the following frequency scoring system sets ranges for each of the scores from zero to five.

**Frequency Scoring Guidelines**

| Score | Description | Time Guideline |
|-------|-------------|----------------|
| 5 | Frequent activity | Weekly |
| 4 | High activity | Quarterly |
| 3 | Normal activity | Annually |
| 2 | Modest activity | Every 2-3 years |
| 1 | Low activity | Every 5+ years |
| 0 | No activity | No historical activity whatsoever |

The same approach can be applied to the severity of a risk, as described in the following severity scoring system. In the sample scoring guidelines, the table notes multiple ways in which to set a zero-to-five score, since it is not always possible to define a risk based on a single set of criteria.

**Severity Scoring Guidelines**

| Score | Description | Sales Reduction | Expense Increase | Order Fulfillment Rate in 24 Hours |
|-------|-------------|-----------------|------------------|------------------------------------|
| 5 | Potentially business threatening | Sales terminated | 50% increase | 0% |
| 4 | Major disruption | 50% decline | 25% increase | 50% |
| 3 | Concerning to stakeholders | 20% decline | 10% increase | 75% |
| 2 | Material impact | 10% decline | 5% increase | 80% |
| 1 | Minor impact | 5% decline | 2% increase | 90% |
| 0 | No impact | < 1% decline | < 0.5% increase | 98% |

Note that in the preceding severity scoring guidelines table, the percentages listed for a sales reduction are higher than the percentages used for an expense increase. The reason for the difference is that the effects of a sales reduction are reduced by the cost of goods sold, which will not occur if there is no sale. This means that the severity scoring will vary, depending on the gross margin that a company earns. For example, a potential sales reduction of 10% may be considered to have a material impact if the contribution margin is high, since most of the sale passes through to profits. Conversely, a potential sales reduction of 10% might be considered to have a minor impact if the contribution margin is relatively low, since only a small part of each sale appears in profits.

## Risk Quantification Issues

Some risks initially appear so vague that it may not seem possible to assign any value to them at all. For example, what is the cost of the loss of a company's reputation? While certainly difficult, it may be possible to estimate these costs by examining what happened to other companies that experienced the same or similar problems in the past. Examples of risks that certainly pose quantification difficulties are:

- Losses from a customer boycott
- Reduced sales from a decline in the perception of a brand
- Difficulty in hiring high-grade employees because of a reputational issue

Other risks are considerably easier to quantify, since a specific action should result in a tightly-defined cost. For example, if a factory is located in a flood plain, flooding damage will be limited to the complete replacement of the factory, along with lost profits from sales that could not be fulfilled from that factory. Similarly, asset expropriation can be tightly defined; the assets located in the at-risk country will be taken.

The cost of some risks will fall midway between the two extremes just noted, and may encompass expenditures that a business has not been accustomed to dealing with in the past. For example, a company dealing with a loss in reputation may need to factor in the cost of a lobbyist, extra security personnel to protect company property, a community relations manager, payments to the local populace, an advertising campaign, a public relations advisor, incentive packages to retain or hire employees, and so forth.

Once risks have been quantified, there may be a temptation to multiply the expected cost range by the probability of occurrence, which results in an expected value. For example, if the probability of an event is 10% and the cost of an unfavorable outcome is $1 million, we multiply the cost by the probability to arrive at an expected value of $100,000. The trouble with the expected value concept is that it tends to hide the sheer size of some risks. For example, a risk may have a cost of $100 million but a probability of only ¼%, so anyone examining the expected value report would reasonably conclude that the risk is worth only $250,000. In reality, management should be made aware of the total projected cost of a risk, even if the risk is small, to see which risks are hefty enough to bring down a business. This means that both the probability and cost information for each risk should be disseminated.

## The Risk Profile

A risk profile is a categorization of the main risks that can impact an organization. A risk profile document is useful for focusing the attention of management on those risks that can cause significant turmoil for the entity, either in terms of financial losses or operational difficulties. The types of categories used can vary by organization. Here are a number of risk categories that might be used:

- *Brand.* Includes issues that can cause the perception of a company's brand to decline, such as a product recall, a marketing flop, bad publicity, negative product reviews, and public squabbles with business partners.

- *Catastrophic*. Primarily includes natural disasters, such as hurricanes, earthquakes, tornadoes, and floods.
- *Environmental*. Includes fines and remediation costs related to pollution, as well as damage to the environment.
- *Financial*. Includes the risks of customer nonpayment, foreign exchange rate variability, capital availability concerns, and employee fraud.
- *Human resources*. Includes the loss of key employees and the lack of properly directive leadership.
- *Industry risk*. Includes factors that can alter the competitive profile of the industry, such as changes in the entire size of the market that the industry serves, the rate at which the industry is consolidating, and the ability of new competitors to enter the market.
- *Information technology*. Includes factors that do not allow an organization to have responsive IT systems, such as being tied to legacy software and having a significant amount of systems downtime. Can also include system breaches that result in the loss of key data.
- *International*. Includes factors caused by doing business in other countries, such as employee kidnappings, terrorist attacks, asset expropriation, political unrest, and sanctions.
- *Legal and regulatory*. Includes new laws or regulatory requirements, such as changes in available tax credits and increased filing requirements for publicly held companies. Can also include internal legal issues, such as being unable to lock down trade secrets.
- *Operational*. Includes factors that impact the ability to produce a sufficient number of quality goods and services, such as inadequate peak capacity, low fulfillment rates, high scrap rates, and processes not being followed.
- *Strategic*. Includes risks arising from the decisions that management makes to follow certain strategic directions. Examples of these risks are bringing new products too late to market, being unable to secure key distribution channels, and selling a product mix that does not attract a sufficient number of customers.

The risk profile document can be combined with the preceding risk rankings chart to yield a good overview of the risks to which a business is subjected. This report can be used as the basis for risk management planning, budgeting, and presentations to the board of directors and the investment community.

## Risk Management Themes

There are several general themes that well-managed businesses usually follow, and which keep them from adopting risky behavior patterns. If the management team adheres to the following concepts, it is much less likely to experience major losses or participate in highly risky, high-return enterprises. These themes are:

- *Deep knowledge of the business.* Risky behavior is much less likely to arise when every employee of a business has a deep knowledge of his or her own responsibilities, and also how the organization as a whole operates. When there is a well-trained work force, many more people can spot anomalies that may lead to losses, and will also recognize the associated risks that accompany new business proposals. This level of detailed knowledge should cover absolutely everyone – from the board of directors down to production-line employees. This level of knowledge can only be obtained through the long-term training of all employees on all aspects of the business. It also requires basic business policies to promote employee retention, such as excellent benefits, a commitment to retain staff during business downturns, and promoting from within. The same concepts should be applied to the internal audit staff.

---

**EXAMPLE**

Creekside Industrial hires a hot new prospect into the purchasing department who comes from a leading university, and who wants to experiment with many new ways to save money for the company. One of her proposals is to use hedging strategies to mitigate swings in the costs of several metals that Creekside uses in its production processes. The idea is interesting, but no one else in the business has any experience with the hedging concept. What steps should Mr. Haley, the purchasing manager, take?

Creekside has had a long-term commitment to ensuring that there is a thorough understanding of every aspect of its business. Since hedging is entirely new, Mr. Haley takes the following steps to reduce the associated risk of hedging:

1. Discusses the matter with the risk management committee and gains their preliminary approval of the concept.
2. Hires a consulting firm to make presentations to the board of directors, risk management committee, and purchasing department regarding the mechanics of the hedging process and the risks that can arise.
3. Retains the consulting firm to engage in a small number of hedging transactions on a pilot basis, instructing the purchasing staff about the process. This includes creating policies and procedures.
4. The consulting firm then switches roles and oversees several purchasing employees as they engage in more hedging transactions and provides corrective advice as needed.
5. The internal audit department is brought in and examines the proposed process flow. The internal audit manager devises several audit procedures that will be conducted periodically to ensure that the hedging process is operating as planned. The external auditors are notified of the hedging initiative and examine the initial process flow, as

well as the internal audit team's proposed examination plans. The external auditors provide advice regarding any issues found.

6. The risk management committee and then the board of directors give their formal approval of the hedging activity, and both request an initial quarterly milestone review meeting to discuss the outcome of initial hedging activities.

7. Hedging activities begin.

Mr. Haley has acted correctly in bringing numerous parties into the discussion of a hedging initiative, while also obtaining expert advice from a third party. He then ensures that the hedging activities are properly described and monitored, and that many people both inside and outside of the purchasing department are made aware of this activity.

The worst action that Mr. Haley could have taken would be to allow the new hire to solely pursue the hedging concept, which would have the dual negative effects of concentrating knowledge of the process with one person, and of creating the risk of an incorrect hedge that might be mistakenly entered into because the individual has no direct experience in hedging transactions.

---

- *Infrastructure commitment.* A proper level of risk management requires deep controls in selected parts of an organization – even if those controls are expensive and/or interfere with the efficient processing of transactions. In a business that focuses excessively on streamlining operations and cutting out costs, it is likely that key controls will be removed, thereby making it more likely that high-loss incidents will occur. This issue is less likely when responsibility over processes and controls is kept away from profit center managers, so there is no temptation to reduce controls in order to increase profits. A strong commitment to infrastructure is especially important when there is a drive to re-engineer processes, since the newly reformulated systems are likely to contain fewer controls than the predecessor systems.

**EXAMPLE**

Celsius Corporation is under significant cost pressure, so the management team has elected to centralize all accounting operations into one location, rather than the current situation, where all four company subsidiaries employ their own accounting departments. The change is expected to yield annual cost savings of $4,000,000, due to reduced headcount and being able to pay software maintenance fees on a single accounting software package.

The projected cost savings are so attractive that the senior management team is pushing for a quick rollout of the new, centralized operation. However, the controller is concerned that the wholesale shutdown of accounting systems will result in key controls being deleted. She asks the internal audit manager to investigate the situation, which results in the following findings:

- The new system has no provision for having local supervisors manually approve employee overtime at the subsidiaries, which presents the risk that overtime will be fraudulently claimed.

- The new system has no provision for comparing supplier invoices to receipt records (which are maintained locally), so there is a risk that false or excessively large supplier invoices will be paid.
- The new system automatically sends electronic invoices to customers, with no provision for a manual proofreading step, as had previously been the case. The company issues extremely complex invoices to its customers, so proofreading is needed to keep customers from rejecting invoices.

The findings are included in the implementation plan for the new system. In addition, the controller asks the internal audit manager to schedule a series of reviews of all aspects of the new system, to see if any other issues arise from the loss of controls.

---

- *Activity boundaries*. Many business transactions can be taken to excess, so it is necessary to set boundaries to limit them. For example, it may be acceptable to write 1,000 insurance policies for flood damage in Louisiana, but writing 100,000 of them will expose an insurer to a potentially massive loss if the Mississippi River overflows its banks. Similarly, it may be unwise to double the amount of credit available to a customer, if the amount of this increase would expose the seller to a large enough bad debt to destroy the business.

---

**EXAMPLE**

The president of Henderson Industrial has retired, so the board of directors conducts a search and hires an outsider, Mr. Blinker. The new president negotiates for an expanded range of authority, which gives him a high level of overriding control over the entire business, with few checks and balances.

After a few months, the chief risk officer notes a number of circumstances in which controls have been overridden by Mr. Blinker, which were specifically allowed when his three-year contract was negotiated. Specifically, he has mandated increased production levels and then offered promotions to distributors to buy goods now. He has also offered much longer payment terms to key customers, and is planning an expansion into a country that all of Henderson's competitors have abandoned due to the level of unrest in that region. Mr. Blinker's reasoning in taking these steps is to boost sales. However, the added sales come at the risk of higher returns from distributors, more bad debts from customers, and outright business failure in the new sales region. In short, the president is accepting much more risk in exchange for increased sales. The risk levels taken on all of these activities exceed the boundaries set by his predecessor, who advocated no channel stuffing, reasonable payment terms, and no foreign sales activity.

The chief risk officer takes his concerns to the audit committee, which brings the matter to the attention of the board of directors. Shortly thereafter, the company issues a press release that Mr. Blinker is leaving the company to pursue other interests.

---

- *Performance targets*. The management team should set reasonable performance targets for a business. By doing so, employees can set a reasonable and sustainable annual pace at which to grow sales. If targets are set too high, and especially if compensation systems match the high targets, then expect employees to engage in increasingly risky behavior, if not outright fraud, in order to meet the imposed targets. The performance targets to be set depend on the stage in the life of a product or business. Early sales may increase at a prodigious growth rate until the market reaches maturity, at which point vastly lower performance targets should be set. This is also a function of the gross sales level of a business – that is, an organization with $1 million in sales may reasonably expect to double its sales in one year, but a $10 billion business is extremely unlikely to duplicate this feat.

---

**EXAMPLE**

Medusa Medical sells a special blend of rapeseed oil through retail stores that specialize in home health care products. Since its founding four years before, the company has experienced 50% average annual sales growth. A venture capital fund has invested several million dollars in the company, in the belief that the business can grow at an even faster rate.

To meet the inflated sales figures that the founder used to attract the venture capitalists, the sales target for the next year is set at a level 80% higher than the year before. To achieve this goal, the company hires an appropriate number of sales representatives, but does not plan on an adequate ramp up period in which to train the new hires. Also, there is an incorrect assumption that additional sales can be squeezed from the existing sales regions, which proves not to be the case. As a result, all of the new hires find that they are falling far behind their sales quotas, and so resort to making sales pitches to financially questionable retailers. The resulting orders trigger a much higher level of bad debt losses than the company had experienced in the past. At year-end, sales do not reach the anticipated levels, while profits actually decline due to the extra costs of the new hires and bad debts.

**EXAMPLE**

In the past year, the price of oil increased to an all-time high, so the senior management team of Franklin Drilling decided to implement a new bonus plan that compensates the entire management team based on the number of new wells drilled from which there is a minimum threshold amount of oil flow per day. The intent is to greatly increase the volume of oil that Franklin can sell in the next year, presumably reaping massive profits. The company plans to invest an average of $2.5 million in each hole drilled.

Seeing massive bonuses in their future, the management group enthusiastically leases land in prime drilling areas and invests in the drilling of dozens of wells. In the meantime, the price of oil plummets. However, the management team continues to drill, since their incentive plan does not account for changes in the price of oil – they are only interested in producing more oil.

By the end of the year, the company has invested over $100 million in new wells and $5 million in bonus payouts, but is forced to cap many of the wells, because the market price of oil now makes it unprofitable to extract the oil.

A better approach would have been to tie overall performance to profitability, since doing so would have accounted for variations in the market price of oil.

## Summary

The development of a system that truly manages risk is not one that only deals with the most obvious risks; and it is not one that continually copies forward the plan from the preceding year. Instead, a high-grade risk management plan is the result of a thoughtful process that continually reexamines a business and its environment, with a particular focus on any changes that may alter the risk profile of the entity. Further, the risk management mindset should be driven deep into the fundamentals of the business, so that it is routinely considered as part of many business decisions.

The internal audit department has a major role to play in the area of risk management. It can engage in a number of assurance engagements to evaluate how well the organization is managing identified risks. It can also conduct consulting activities to provide advice concerning problems with and recommendations for improvements to the risk management system. Under no circumstances should internal auditors be tasked with the management of risk-related activities, since this would impede their ability to conduct assurance engagements.

# Chapter 4
# Business Processes

## Introduction

The internal auditor needs to understand which business processes are the most critical to the functioning of a business, as well as which ones have the greatest impact on the objectives of the organization. Doing so requires the use of a ranking system for all business processes, so that one can identify which ones require detailed analysis. In this chapter, we cover the nature of business processes, risk factor analysis, and the various tools available for documenting targeted processes. This information is essential for the development of an audit plan that focuses on the most important business processes.

## Business Processes

A foundation for the proper governance of an organization is a well-thought-out set of business processes that are closely adhered to by employees. A *business process* is a set of connected tasks that result in the completion of a goal. There should always be one or more inputs to a business process, which results in some form of output; this frequently results in a sequential series of processes, where the output from one process serves as an input to another process. A core set of business processes is found in all organizations, but many are custom-designed to meet the needs of a firm's industry-specific operations. Examples of common business processes are:

- Develop a corporate strategy
- Acquire funding
- Acquire or construct fixed assets
- Collect payments from customers
- Design products
- Conduct marketing campaigns
- Pay employees and contractors
- Pay suppliers
- Process product returns
- Produce financial statements
- Purchase inventory and schedule its use
- Recruit, hire, and train employees
- Remit taxes to the government
- Sell goods and services

For example, an essential business process is paying employees. Someone needs to compile the hours worked by each employee, multiply these hours by the person's pay rate, deduct taxes and other items, and process payments. The inputs to the process are hours worked, pay rates, tax rates, and deductions, while the outputs are paychecks and tax remittances.

A variation on the concept is the *project*, which involves a complex series of activities that result in a unique outcome. For example, an oil exploration company is in the business of investigating geological data for signs of oil deposits, procuring leases on promising parcels of land, and conducting drilling operations. There are certainly common elements within these activities that are duplicated on successive projects, but the activities must be modified to fit the circumstances of each project.

When a business has a comprehensive set of interlocking business processes, it is much easier for the board of directors to ensure that the organization will adhere to its governance framework. This means that the operability and risk profiles of those business processes are a significant concern for the internal audit manager, who must have a detailed understanding of how these processes work. In order to understand a process, the internal audit department should compile detailed documentation for it, which we will describe later in this chapter.

Before embarking on the massive task of documenting all business processes, the internal audit manager should identify those that are key to the accomplishment of the company's objectives. It is more critical that these processes function correctly, since they have such a direct impact on the firm's strategic plan. This prioritization is quite useful for focusing attention on a few dozen processes out of the hundreds or thousands of processes currently in operation. Thus, the product design process may be considered more critical than the janitorial services process, since the development of profitable products on a timely basis is essential to the fiscal well-being of the organization.

The same approach can be used to apply the key risks of the business (as described in the preceding chapter) to each process. If a process is closely linked to a business risk, then it is a prime candidate for review by the internal audit department. This is the case to an even greater extent when a process is closely associated with *several* business risks. A variation on the concept is to review each process in terms of a standard set of risks, resulting in a risk score for each one. A process with a high risk score is definitely a candidate for an internal auditing assurance engagement.

## EXAMPLE

Arbitrary Outcomes is an international manufacturer of slot machines. Its internal audit department has identified more than 500 business processes within the organization, and wants to sort them based on risk, to decide which ones to document and schedule for audits. It derives the following risk factor table to conduct the analysis, where weightings are assigned to each of the risk factors to emphasize their importance:

| Risk Factor | Risk Options | Score | × Weight | Weighted Score |
|---|---|---|---|---|
| Complexity | 1 – Simple process<br>2 – Requires multiple people<br>3 – Highly complex, multiple participants | | 5 | |
| Impact on the firm | 1 – Affects < 2% of company activities<br>2 – Affects 2-20% of company activities<br>3 – Affects > 20% of company activities | | 2 | |
| Assets at risk | 1 – Less than $250,000<br>2 - $250,000 to $750,000<br>3 – More than $750,000 | | 1 | |
| Stable internal controls | 1 – Robust, well-defined internal controls<br>2 – Minor changes in the recent past<br>3 – Significant changes in the recent past | | 2 | |
| Effective internal controls | 1 – No compliance issues found in last audit<br>2 – Some control failures found, not in last audit<br>3 – Significant control failures in the last audit | | 3 | |
| Process changes | 1 – No changes to the process/personnel in past year<br>2 – Some changes to the process/personnel in past year<br>3 – Major changes to the process/personnel in past year | | 4 | |
| | **Risk Score:** | | | |

The internal audit staff applies this risk factor table to the product design process, with the following results:

| Risk Factor | Risk Options | Score | × Weight | Weighted Score |
|---|---|---|---|---|
| Complexity | 1 – Simple process<br>2 – Requires multiple people<br>3 – Highly complex, multiple participants | 3 | 5 | 15 |
| Impact on the firm | 1 – Affects < 2% of company activities<br>2 – Affects 2-20% of company activities<br>3 – Affects > 20% of company activities | 3 | 2 | 6 |
| Assets at risk | 1 – Less than $250,000<br>2 - $250,000 to $750,000<br>3 – More than $750,000 | 1 | 1 | 1 |
| Stable internal controls | 1 – Robust, well-defined internal controls<br>2 – Minor changes in the recent past<br>3 – Significant changes in the recent past | 2 | 2 | 4 |
| Effective internal controls | 1 – No compliance issues found in last audit<br>2 – Some control failures found, not in last audit<br>3 – Significant control failures in the last audit | 1 | 3 | 3 |
| Process changes | 1 – No changes to the process/personnel in past year<br>2 – Some changes to the process/personnel in past year<br>3 – Major changes to the process/personnel in past year | 2 | 4 | 8 |
| | **Risk Score:** | | | 37 |

**Tip:** One way to schedule internal audit projects is in declining order by their risk scores, until all department resources for the planning period have been consumed. Another option is to schedule more frequent audits for those processes with the highest risk scores; thus, a process with a high risk score might trigger an annual audit, while a process with a low risk score might only be audited once every five years.

## The Need for Systems Documentation

In addition to the needs of the internal audit department, there are multiple reasons why a business should have adequate documentation of its systems. They are as follows:

- *Audits.* Systems documentation is commonly used for outside auditors, who need to understand how systems and their related controls operate. This information is needed to develop an opinion about the robustness of a company's system of internal controls. This is especially important for a publicly held company, which is required by the Sarbanes-Oxley Act of 2002 to establish an adequate system of internal controls, whose effectiveness must be evaluated by its auditors.

- *Controls.* Proper documentation can be used to highlight where controls may be lacking in a system, or where there are overlapping controls that could present opportunities for the selective reduction of controls.
- *System development or selection.* The documentation for an existing system can form the basis for the development of systems configuration documents for a proposed new system that needs to contain many of the capabilities of the old system.
- *Training.* Systems documentation can be used as the basis for training materials for system users. This is especially effective if the systems documentation is regularly updated to reflect changes in the underlying systems, and the revised documentation is then used to update training materials.

The preceding points become more urgent as a business grows in size, since its systems gradually increase in complexity and would otherwise be excessively difficult to understand.

## Business Process Documentation Activities

How does the internal auditor document a business process? The first source of information should be the process owner. This is the person who is responsible for how the process functions on a daily basis. This person either directly engages in each task within the process or supervises people who do. The process owner may also have some documentation of the process, with varying degrees of sophistication. Though this documentation can be of assistance, one should not assume that it accurately reflects the current process flow (which may have changed over time). Instead, interview those actively involved in the process, noting inputs to and outputs from the process, and the nature of the transformational activities conducted by each person.

To gain an understanding of which elements of a business process are considered the most essential to management, the auditor should make inquiries about the nature of any associated measurement systems. Metrics that are being compiled and forwarded to management frequently, and especially those which trigger immediate management actions, are clearly considered to be associated with essential aspects of a process, and so should be thoroughly investigated. For example, if inventory shrinkage is closely monitored at a brewery, this is a clear indication that fluid loss during the brewing process is a significant concern for management, and so warrants particular attention to documentation of the brewing process.

Once the initial round of interviews is complete, the auditor should document the results in a flowchart (as described in the next section) and then review it with the interviewees. This may result in several iterations before the flowchart accurately reflects how a business process actually functions.

## Flowcharts

A *flowchart* is a diagram that graphically describes a business process. Each step in a process is represented by a box or some similar graphic, which contains text that briefly describes the step. It helps an internal auditor to visualize what is going on in a system, though the graphical nature of the presentation may not be that useful when a process is unusually complex. Flowcharts can be subdivided into the following classifications:

- *Document flowcharts.* Portrays the flow of documents through a system, including where they are created, distributed, and disposed of.
- *Data flowcharts.* Depicts the flow of data through a system.
- *System flowcharts.* Represents the relationships between the input, processing, and outputs of a system.

Given their role in clarifying processes, it can make sense to minimize the number of symbols used. The four symbols appearing in the following exhibit should be sufficient for most applications, though there are many other symbols available that can be used, portraying communication links, manual operations, electronic output, computer processing, and so forth.

**Standard Flowchart Symbols**

| Symbol | Discussion |
|---|---|
| | **Process:** This is the primary symbol used in a flowchart. State each step within a process box. It is possible that a simplified flowchart will contain no other shapes. |
| | **Decision:** This is used when a decision will result in a different process flow. The decision symbol can be overused. Try to restrict its usage to no more than two per flowchart. Otherwise, the flowchart will appear overly complex. If more decision symbols are needed, consider subdividing a flowchart into multiple documents. |
| | **Document:** This symbol is particularly useful for showing where an input form is used to collect information for a process, though it can also represent a report generated *by* a process. |
| | **Database:** This symbol is used less frequently, and shows when information is extracted from or stored in a computer database. In most cases, the use of a database can be implied without cluttering up a flowchart with the symbol. |

An example of a flowchart that documents the handling of cash receipts from customers appears in the following exhibit. The flowchart is clearly much simpler to understand than the following narrative of the same process, requiring only a few moments for a user to gain an understanding of the underlying process. The narrative description is:

1. **Accept and record cash.** If the business is paid by a customer in cash, record the payment in a cash register. If there is no cash register (as may be the case in a low-volume sales environment), the sales clerk instead fills out a two-part sales receipt, gives a copy to the customer, and retains the other copy.
2. **Match receipts to cash.** Compare the amount of cash received to either the cash register receipt total or the total of all sales receipt copies, and investigate any differences. Complete a reconciliation form for any differences found.
3. **Aggregate and post receipt information.** Summarize the information in the cash register and post this information to the general ledger as a sale and cash receipt. If the cash register is linked to the company's accounting system and is tracking individual sales, then sales are being recorded automatically, as is the reduction of goods in the inventory records. If sales clerks are manually completing sales receipts, summarize the information in the sales receipts and record the sales and any related inventory reductions in the general ledger.
4. **Deposit cash.** Prepare a bank deposit slip, retain a copy, and enclose the original slip along with all cash in a locked container for transport to the bank. After counting the cash, the bank issues a receipt stating the amount it has received.
5. **Match to deposit slip.** Compare the copy of the deposit slip to the bank receipt, and investigate any differences. A variation is to compare the cash receipts journal to the bank receipt.

## Cash Receipts Flowchart

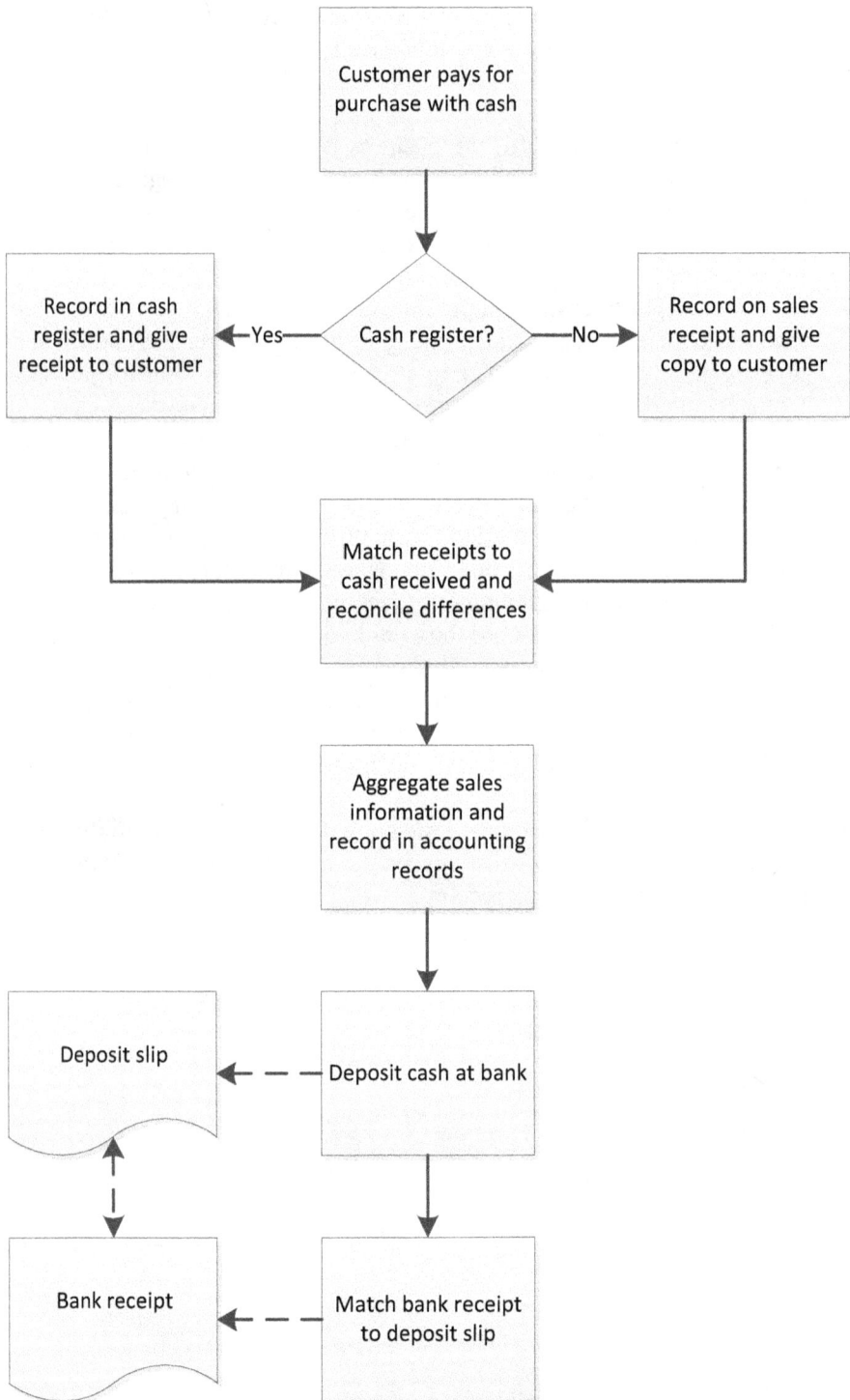

Customer pays for purchase with cash

Cash register?

Yes — Record in cash register and give receipt to customer

No — Record on sales receipt and give copy to customer

Match receipts to cash received and reconcile differences

Aggregate sales information and record in accounting records

Deposit cash at bank

Deposit slip

Match bank receipt to deposit slip

Bank receipt

One should keep the following best practices in mind when developing flowcharts:

- *Standardize the flow.* The information in a flowchart should begin at the top or in the top left corner and proceed to the bottom or bottom right corner, thereby establishing a standard flow.
- *Minimize information.* Ideally, a flowchart should contain much less information than a narrative description of a system, so that only the highlights of the basic process steps are revealed.
- *Eliminate insignificant items.* Strip out minor steps that are rarely used. It makes more sense to focus on those aspects of the system that are used on a repetitive basis.
- *Terminate the flowchart.* If any activities or documents continue off the bottom of the flowchart, identify the name of the flowchart in which the description continues. Otherwise, the reader does not gain a complete understanding of the underlying process.
- *Conduct a walkthrough.* Conduct a joint walkthrough of the flowchart with someone else who is knowledgeable in the targeted system, to see if there are any errors or omissions that need to be corrected.

## Business Process Diagrams

A business process diagram (BPD) graphically depicts the flow of business processes. The intent is to give readers a simplified, easy-to-understand overview of a process. A minimal number of symbols are used in a BPD, usually just a rectangle to describe activities, and arrows to indicate the flow of activities. The diagram reads from left to right and from top to bottom. A sample BPD for the purchase of goods appears in the following example.

When preparing a BPD, one should keep in mind the best practices noted previously for flowcharts. In addition, consider the following:

- *Simplify the format.* Since this is a high-level diagram, simplify it as much as possible by only using two columns. The first column states who is engaged in an activity, while the second column describes their activities.
- *Stay high level.* A BPD is constructed at such a high level that there is no need to delve into the details of exactly which documents are used, or which software is employed to process data. This means that a BPD is much less likely to require revision as certain aspects of a system are altered over time.

## Purchasing Business Process Diagram

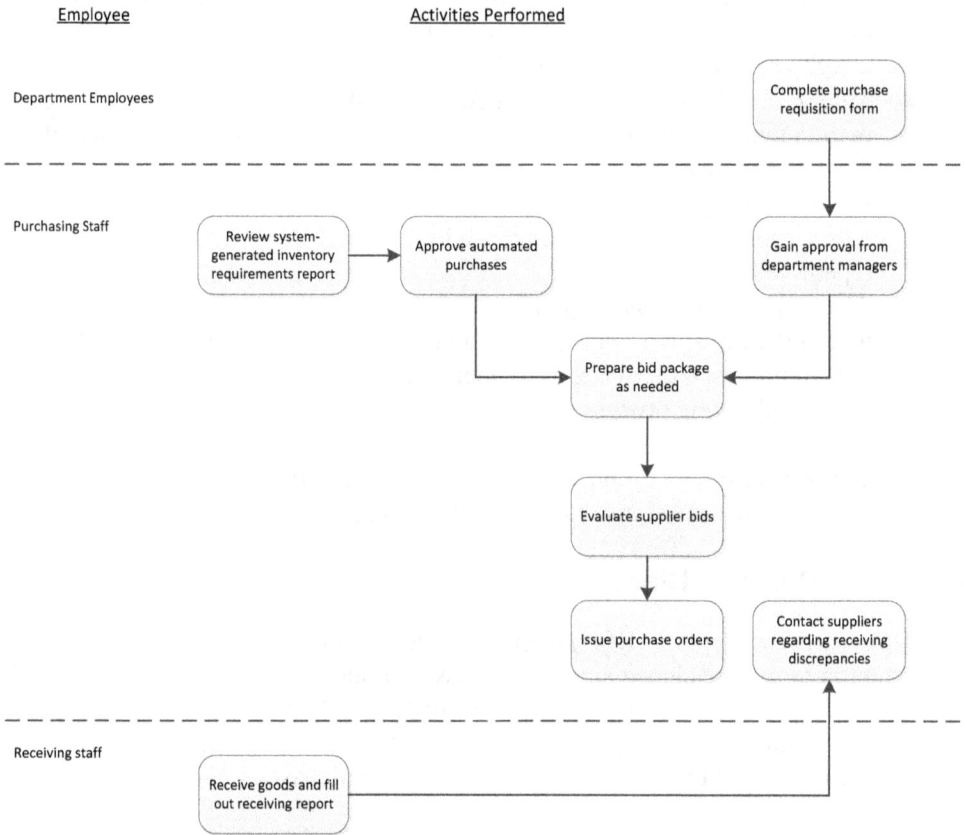

Employee        Activities Performed

Department Employees — Complete purchase requisition form

Purchasing Staff — Review system-generated inventory requirements report → Approve automated purchases → Gain approval from department managers

Prepare bid package as needed

Evaluate supplier bids

Issue purchase orders — Contact suppliers regarding receiving discrepancies

Receiving staff — Receive goods and fill out receiving report

# The Role of Internal Auditing

The internal audit department can be quite useful to an organization in identifying the most important business processes, especially in terms of their impact on various risks impacting the organization. When risks are spotted, the auditing staff can educate managers about where risks are located within their areas of responsibility and the likely impact on the organization in the event of a failure. This can lead to recommendations for adjustments to the system of controls associated with a process, either to mitigate the current risk level or to dial back excessive controls.

Internal auditing can be of particular use to management during periods when new initiatives are being rolled out or current ones scaled back, since this may involve changes to business processes and the risks associated with them.

Auditors can also provide advice about whether the existing performance metrics for processes are sufficiently effective, or if alternative metrics should be considered. This may include changes to the timing of metrics reports and the level of detail provided to management.

## Summary

The approaches to business process analysis and systems documentation described in this chapter are quite useful for the internal auditor, since they can provide a basic understanding of a business process in short order, from which an audit program can be developed. When combined with an analysis of the risk identification, quantification, and ranking systems described in the preceding chapter, the auditor can gain a solid understanding of the precise points within an organization that are most in need of review, and which should therefore be included in the annual audit plan for the department.

# Chapter 5
# Internal Controls

## Introduction

A system of internal controls is an interlocking set of activities that are layered onto the normal operating procedures of an organization, with the intent of safeguarding assets, minimizing errors, and ensuring that operations are conducted in an approved manner. Another way of looking at internal control is that these activities are needed to mitigate the amount and types of risk to which a firm is subjected. Controls are also useful for consistently producing reliable financial statements.

Internal control comes at a price, which is that control activities frequently slow down the natural process flow of a business, which can reduce its overall efficiency. Consequently, the development of a system of internal controls requires management to balance risk reduction with efficiency. This process can sometimes result in management accepting a certain amount of risk in order to create a strategic profile that allows a company to compete more effectively, even if it suffers occasional losses because controls have been deliberately reduced.

## The Proper Balance of Control Systems

A person who has been trained in control systems will likely want to install every possible control, and will then feel satisfied that he or she has saved the company from an impending failure. Those on the receiving end of these controls have a different opinion of the situation, which is that controls slow down transactions, require more staff, and have the same general effect on a business as pouring sand into the gas tank of a car. Because of these radically differing views of the utility of control systems, it is useful to adopt a set of controls that are based on the following points:

- *Risk – monetary*. If a control can prevent a large loss, such as one that could bankrupt a business, then it makes sense to install it, as long as the probability of the event is reasonably high. For example, having two people involved in every wire transfer transaction is a reasonable precaution, given the amount of funds that could be transferred out in a single wire transfer. Conversely, if a control can never save more than a few dollars (such as locking the office supply cabinet), it is entirely likely that the sheer annoyance caused by the control greatly outweighs any possible savings to be achieved from it.
- *Risk – financial statements*. A business must understand its performance, and it can only do so with reliable financial statements. Consequently, controls over recordkeeping should be among the most comprehensive in the company. However, this does not necessarily call for an oppressive amount of controls in those areas where the amounts involved are essentially immaterial to the financial statements.

- *Repetitiveness.* Only install comprehensive controls for those transactions that a business will engage in on a recurring basis. For example, if a company sells equipment to a foreign customer once a year, and wants to hedge the outstanding receivable, a once-a-year transaction does not require an elaborate control system (unless the receivable is for a large amount – see the preceding point about risk). Thus, it behooves a business to concentrate on a finely-tuned set of controls for the 20% of its processes that make up 80% of its business (the Pareto Principle). Of the remaining 80% of the company's processes, those items involving the most inherent risk should be the prime candidates for strong controls.
- *Offsetting controls.* It may be acceptable to have weak controls in one part of a business, as long as there are offsetting controls elsewhere. For example, it may not be necessary to have someone sign checks, as long as all purchases are initiated with an authorizing purchase order. This concept can be used to great effect if there is a good business reason to keep one business process running as smoothly as possible (i.e., without controls), with offsetting controls in a less noticeable part of the business.
- *Cost.* The cost of controls must be balanced against the expected reduction in risk. This is not a simple calculation to make, for it can be quite difficult to estimate the reduction of risk that will be achieved by implementing a control. One approach to quantifying risk is to multiply the risk percentage by the exposure to the business, which is known as the *expected loss*. See the following example.

    Conversely, it is easy enough to measure the labor cost and other factors required to implement and maintain a control, so there is a tendency for businesses to focus on the up-front cost of a control and downplay the savings that may or may not arise from having the control. The result tends to be a control level that is lower than it should be.

---

**EXAMPLE**

High Noon Armaments operates a payroll system that pays employees on a semi-monthly basis. When there are a significant number of data errors in the payroll, High Noon's payroll manager requires that the payroll be run again, at a cost of $5,000.

The payroll manager is considering the installation of an automated data validation software package that is expected to reduce the payroll data error rate from 8% to 1%, at a software rental cost of $250 per payroll. The cost–benefit analysis is:

- *No data validation.* There is an 8% chance of incurring a $5,000 payroll reprocessing cost, which is an expected loss of $400 ($5,000 exposure × 8% risk) per payroll.
- *Data validation.* There is a 1% chance of incurring a $5,000 payroll reprocessing cost, which is an expected loss of $50 ($5,000 exposure × 1% risk) per payroll. There is also a charge of $250 per payroll for the software rental cost.

Thus, there is a reduction of $350 in the expected loss if the control is implemented, against which there is a control cost of $250. This results in a net gain of $100 per payroll by using the control. Changes in the estimated probabilities can have a significant impact on the outcome of this analysis.

---

The resulting system should be one where some failures will still occur, but either in such small amounts that they do not place the business at risk, or where the probability of occurrence is very low. It is difficult to maintain this balance between controls and operational effectiveness over time, seeing that a growing business is constantly in a state of flux, expanding some lines of business, curtailing others, and installing any number of new systems. It is the job of the controller to watch the interaction of these processes with existing control systems, and know when it is an acceptable risk to pare back some controls, while introducing new ones elsewhere. The internal audit department can act in a consulting role here, to present the controller with the pluses and minuses associated with changes to existing controls.

It is quite common to see a control system that lags behind the current state of its processes, usually due to inattention by the controller. This means that some controls are so antiquated as to be essentially meaningless (while still annoying the staff), while new systems are devoid of controls, and will only see new ones when a system failure occurs.

In summary, there is a balance between the system of controls and the efficient operation of a business that is difficult to manage. A good controller will understand the needs of employees to keep operations efficient, and so should be willing to subsist in some areas on control systems that may appear rather skimpy, as long as the tradeoff is between a notable improvement in efficiency and the risk of only modest losses that would have been prevented by controls.

## Control Principles

There are a number of principles to keep in mind when constructing a system of controls for a business. These principles are frequently the difference between a robust control system and one that appears adequate on paper, but which never seems to work in practice. The principles are:

- *Separation of duties*. The separation of duties involves assigning different parts of a process to different people, so that collusion would be required for someone to commit fraud. For example, one person opens the mail and records a list of the checks received, while a different person records them in the accounting system and a third person deposits the checks. By separating these tasks, it is much more difficult for someone to (for example) remove a check from the incoming mail, record a receivables credit in the accounting system to cover his tracks, and cash the check into his own account. Unfortunately, there is a major downside to the separation of duties, which is that shifting tasks among multiple people interferes with the efficiency of a process. Consequently, this control principle should only be used at the minimum level needed to establish the desired level of control – too much of it is not cost-effective.

- *Process integration.* Controls should be so thoroughly intertwined with business transactions that it is impossible for employees *not* to perform them as part of their daily activities. This level of integration substantially reduces the incidence of errors and the risk of fraud. An example of proper process integration with a control is running all produced items past a fixed bar code scanning station on a conveyor belt, to ensure that all completed goods are recorded. The information is collected without the staff having to do anything. An example of minimal process integration that will likely result in frequent control problems is requiring employees to record this information by hand on a paper form.

- *Management support.* The management team must make it abundantly clear to employees that it thoroughly supports the system of controls. This does not mean that a general statement of ethics is included in the employee manual. Instead, it means that management takes the time to explain controls to employees, is highly visible in investigating control breaches, and takes sufficient remedial action to make it clear to the entire staff that controls are to be taken seriously. Management also does not override its own controls, nor does it set performance standards that are so difficult to attain that employees would be forced to circumvent controls in order to meet the standards.

- *Responsibility.* Someone should be assigned responsibility for every control, and receive regular updates on the status of those controls. It is also useful if the status of their controls is noted in their compensation reviews, and has a direct impact on their pay.

- *Conscientious application.* Employees cannot treat controls in a perfunctory manner. Instead, there should be a culture that encourages the close examination of control breaches to determine what went wrong, and how the system can be adjusted to reduce the risk that the same issue will occur again. This level of conscientious behavior must be encouraged by the management team through constant reinforcement of the message that the system of controls is important. It also requires the availability of communication channels through which employees can anonymously report suspected improprieties.

- *Systems knowledge.* It is impossible to expect employees to conscientiously inspect controls unless they already know how systems operate. This calls for the ongoing training of employees to ensure that they thoroughly understand all aspects of the systems with which they are involved. This requires not only an initial training session for new employees, but also reminder sessions that are timed to coincide with any changes in processes and related controls, as well as thorough documentation of the systems. A good level of systems knowledge may call for the use of procedures, training materials, and a core group of trainers.

- *Error reporting.* It is impossible to know if a control is functioning properly unless there is a system in place for reporting control breaches. This may be a report generated by a computer system, but it may also call for open communications channels with employees, customers, and suppliers to solicit any errors that have been found. In this latter case, error reporting is strongly supported by a management group that is clearly interested in spotting errors and correcting them in a way that does not cast blame on those reporting the information. In addition, errors should be communicated all the way up through the organization to the audit committee and board of directors, who can enforce the establishment of enhanced controls.

- *Staffing.* There must be an adequate number of employees on hand to operate controls. Otherwise, there will be great pressure to avoid manual controls, since they take too much time to complete. This is actually a profitability issue, since a business experiencing losses is more likely to cut back on staffing, which in turn impacts the control system.

- *Outlier analysis.* Most businesses create control systems to deal with problems they have seen in the past, or which have been experienced elsewhere in the industry. They rarely create controls designed to mitigate outlier issues – that is, problems that occur very infrequently. The sign of a great control system is one in which employees take the time to examine the control system from a high level, and in light of the current and future business environment, to see if there are any outlier events that present a risk of loss in sufficiently large amounts to warrant the addition of controls. This outlier analysis requires excellent knowledge of the industry and a perceptive view of the direction in which it is headed.

Of the principles just noted, management support is the most crucial. Without it, a system of controls is like a building with no supporting framework – the entire structure crashes to the ground if there is any pressure placed upon it at all. For example, the control system may appear to have proper separation of duties, but this makes no difference if the management team ignores these separations for transactions that it has an interest in ramming through the system.

## The Failings of Internal Controls

A well-constructed system of internal controls can certainly be of assistance to a business, but controls suffer from several conceptual failings. They are:

- *Assured profitability.* No control system on the planet can assure a business of earning a profit. Controls may be able to detect or even avoid some losses, but if a business is inherently unprofitable, there is nothing that a control system can do to repair the situation. Profitability is, to a large extent, based on product quality, marketplace positioning, price points, and other factors that are not related to control systems.

- *Fair financial reporting.* A good control system can go a long ways toward the production of financial statements that fairly present the financial results and position of a business, but this is by no means guaranteed. There will always be outlier or low probability events that will evade the best control system, or there may be employees who conspire to evade the control system.

- *Judgment basis*. Manual controls rely upon the judgment of the people operating them. If a person engages in a control activity and makes the wrong judgment call (such as a bad decision to extend credit to a customer), then the control may have functioned but the outcome was still a failure. Thus, controls can fail if the judgment of the people operating them is poor.
- *Determined fraudulent behavior*. Controls are typically designed to catch fraudulent behavior by an individual who is acting alone. They are much less effective when the management team itself overrides controls, or when several employees collude to engage in fraud. In these cases, it is quite possible to skirt completely around the control system.

Thus, the owners, managers, and employees of a business should view its controls not as an absolute failsafe that will protect the business, but rather as something designed to *increase the likelihood* that operational goals will be achieved, its financial reports can be relied upon, and that it is complying with the relevant laws and regulations.

## Preventive and Detective Controls

When considering the proper balance of controls that a business needs, also consider the types of controls being installed. A *preventive control* is one that keeps a control breach from occurring. This type of control is highly prized, since it has a direct impact on cost reduction. Another type of control is the *detective control*. This control is useful, but only detects a control breach after it has occurred; thus, its main use is in making management aware of a problem that must be fixed.

A control system needs to have a mix of preventive and detective controls. Even though preventive controls are considered more valuable, they also tend to be more intrusive in the functioning of key business processes. Also, they are installed to address specific control issues that management is already aware of. Management also needs a liberal helping of detective controls, which can be used to spot problems that management was *not* aware of. Thus, a common occurrence is to throw out a web of detective controls that occasionally haul in a new type of problem, for which management installs a preventive control.

In short, a mix of the two types of controls is needed, where there may be no ideal solution. Instead, there may be a range of possible configurations within which an internal auditor would consider a control system to be effective.

## Manual and Automated Controls

If a control is operated by the computer system through which business transactions are recorded, this is considered to be an *automated control*. If a control requires someone to manually perform it, this is considered a *manual control*. Automated controls are always preferred, since it is impossible to avoid them. Conversely, manual controls can be easily avoided, simply by forgetting to enact them.

Examples of automated controls are:

- A limit check in a payroll data entry screen that does not allow you to enter more hours in a work week than the total number of hours in a week.
- An address reviewer in the vendor master file that does not allow you to enter an address without the correct zip code.
- An error checker in the inventory database that does not allow an inventory deduction that would otherwise result in a negative inventory balance.

Several examples of manual controls are:

- Requiring a second signature on a check payment that exceeds a certain amount.
- Requiring the review of the final payroll register by a supervisor.
- Requiring the completion of a monthly bank reconciliation.

The best controls are ones that are preventive (see the preceding section) and automated, since they actively prevent errors from occurring and are very difficult to avoid.

## Constructing a System of Controls

The preceding discussion has revolved around the general concept of controls and the principles that should underlie them. But how does a business actually create a system of controls? What are the nuts and bolts of building a system? The primary steps are:

1. *Understand the new system.* Work with the systems analysts who have designed the new system to understand what it is designed to do, and each step in the process flow. This may call for the use of flowcharts and walkthroughs of test transactions. The result may be a formal report describing the system, probably including a preliminary set of procedures.
2. *Explore possible control breaches.* Work with the internal and external auditors, department managers, and systems analysts to estimate where control breaches are most likely to arise in the prospective system.
3. *Quantify possible control breaches.* Estimate the number of occurrences of each type of control breach, the maximum and most likely amounts that a control breach would cost, and their impact on customers and other key company performance metrics.
4. *Design controls.* Based on the quantification of control breaches, design controls that will cost-effectively mitigate risks and be so thoroughly integrated into the underlying process that they will be as robust as possible.
5. *Implement the controls.* Install the controls, along with all necessary documentation, forms, systems, and training, and oversee the initial rollout to ensure that it is operating as planned.
6. *Test the system.* A system of controls does not necessarily operate as planned, perhaps due to a misperception of how the underlying system operates, a bad

control design, technology issues, poor employee training, and so on. To detect these issues, test the system of controls by feeding incorrect transactions into it, and see if the controls detect the transactions. If not, adjust the controls and repeat the exercise as many times as necessary.

7. *Conduct a post-implementation review.* All systems change over time, so expect control redundancy and gaps to appear as systems change. Systems should be reviewed at least once a year, and more frequently if there have been major changes, to see if the existing system of controls should be adjusted. This task may be most easily handled by the internal audit department.

In a larger company, it may be cost-effective to hire a controls analyst who deals with these matters on a full-time basis. In a smaller enterprise, it is more likely that this work will be handled by the controller, who might consider outsourcing it to a consultant.

## Special Case – Employee Turnover

A high level of employee turnover presents a particular problem for the control environment, for controls knowledge weakens with the departure of each successive group of employees. Eventually, employees no longer understand the full breadth of business systems, nor why controls are used. Instead, they are only aware of the particular controls for which they are responsible, and which they were instructed in as part of their abbreviated training. This problem is particularly pernicious when systems and controls are poorly documented, and when those with the most seniority (and presumed knowledge of operations) are the first to leave.

The likely result of a continuing series of employee departures is a gradual decline in the use of manual controls. Also, since employees do not know why controls are being used, they are less likely to be conscientious in pursuing any control breaches found. In addition, business processes will change over time, while controls will no longer change with them. The overall result is a control system that may appear on the surface to be reliable, but which in fact can no longer be relied upon.

## Special Case – Rapid Growth

When a business grows at a high rate of speed, it encounters the same problems found with a high rate of employee turnover. The problem is that the knowledge of business processes and control systems is centered on the core group of original employees, and must be passed along rapidly to an ever-expanding group of employees. The risk in this situation is that controls knowledge will be so ephemeral among newer employees that the same system of controls operated by new employees will be substantially less effective than the same system operated by longer-term employees.

The reduced effectiveness of a control system in this environment can be mitigated through the following actions:

- *System replication.* When there is a high rate of growth, there is no way to accommodate local variations on the basic control system, since each one must be separately documented. Instead, management must settle upon one control system, and replicate it throughout the business in a rigid manner. Such a system is much easier to replicate as the business continues to grow.

- *Written procedures.* When there are too many new employees to be properly trained in person, the fallback approach is to construct written procedures that are as thorough as possible. New employees can use these materials to learn more about controls, and they can also be used as training materials.

- *Training.* It is critically important to have a formal training program in a fast growth environment, since new employees can be rotated through it quickly, and they can all be taught exactly the same material. This allows for a considerable amount of uniformity, which is useful for replicating the same control system throughout a company.

- *Employee dispersion.* No matter how well new employees may be trained, they do not yet fully understand why the control system has been constructed in its present form. To lend credence to the current system, it may be necessary to disperse the original group of employees among the various company locations, where they can provide newer employees with a historical perspective on the control system.

Even the recommendations noted here may not be sufficient. If it becomes apparent that the incidence of control breaches is increasing over time, it may be necessary to slow the rate of company growth until the experience level of the employees has increased sufficiently to operate systems in a competent manner. Thus, the level of control difficulties may determine the pace of further expansion.

## Terminating Controls

Controls tend to slow down the flow of transactions within a business and result in extra costs, and so should only be used when there is a clear need for them. In addition, controls should only be retained for as long as the processes with which they are associated are unchanged. If a process is altered, the linked controls may no longer be needed, but are still retained because no one thought to remove them. The result is likely to be an excessive number of controls and a lower level of process efficiency than should be the case.

Another concern is that too many controls can restrict the ability of employees to take responsibility for their actions. Instead, there is a tendency to adhere to the rules, no matter what, in order to avoid taking responsibility. Eventually, an organization with too many controls becomes hopelessly bureaucratic and calcified, and nearly incapable of enacting any useful changes.

To avoid a burdensome number of controls, it is useful to periodically examine the current system of controls and see if any should be removed. This can be done in the following ways:

- *Review at process change.* Whenever there is a change to a process, incorporate into the process flow analysis a review of all controls built into the process. Doing so may point out that specific controls can be eliminated, or replaced by other controls that are more cost-effective.

- *Review on scheduled date.* Even if there have been no process changes, conduct a comprehensive controls review on a scheduled date, such as once a year. This review may pick up on minor process changes that have been implemented but not formally noted. This approach also allows for consideration of new, more technologically-advanced controls that were not available in previous years.

---

**Tip:** Never review a control in isolation from the other controls in a process, since the entire set of controls may provide backup coverage for each other. Deleting one control may weaken a control issue elsewhere in the business process.

---

No matter which approach is used, it may also make sense to bring in a controls specialist to review existing systems and recommend which controls can be terminated. By doing so, the company gains the benefit of someone who has seen a broad range of controls in many other companies, and who therefore has more experience upon which to base recommendations for changes. The report of this consultant can also be used as justification for changes to the system of controls.

If controls are to be terminated, be sure to discuss the changes thoroughly with the controller and chief financial officer, as well as the company's audit committee. These people may feel that a control should be retained, despite the dictates of efficiency, in order to provide some additional risk reduction.

The termination of a control should not be a special event. Instead, it is an ongoing part of the alterations that a company makes as it changes its business processes to meet the demands of the market.

## The Role of Internal Auditing

It is the job of the internal audit department to conduct assessments of a company's system of internal controls. This needs to be an ongoing series of evaluations that vary in their scope and frequency, depending on an assessment of the risks that each control is designed to mitigate. The internal audit manager summarizes any deficiencies found and discusses them with management and the board of directors, as necessary. These deficiencies may involve the controls themselves or problems with any other monitoring systems that management uses to oversee the system of internal controls, such as ongoing control reviews by management.

The internal audit manager is especially interested in locating any major deficiencies in the system of internal controls. A *major deficiency* is any internal control deficiency that severely reduces the likelihood that a business can achieve its objectives. Given their nature, major deficiencies should be communicated to management and the board of directors at once, so that remedial action can be taken to ensure that company objectives can still be attained. Thereafter, internal auditors should monitor the identified deficiencies to see if they have been corrected.

In addition to its assessment function, the internal audit department can provide assistance in the following areas:

- Assist management in creating a culture of ethical behavior that supports a strong system of internal controls.
- Assist management in creating a process for spotting and fixing internal control deficiencies.
- Assist management in devising a framework for assessing the design and operation of a system of internal controls.
- Inform management of any emerging issues and regulations pertaining to the effectiveness of the firm's system of internal controls.
- Provide training about internal controls to employees throughout the organization.

## Summary

A key point to take away from this chapter is that there is no boilerplate system of controls that can be inserted into a company. Instead, the control system must be fashioned to meet the risk profile of a business, while accepting minor losses in areas where it is more important to pare back on controls in favor of having more efficient business processes. Consequently, it takes a deep knowledge of a company's processes to set up and continually tweak a system of controls that yields the proper blend of risk aversion and business performance.

Even if a correct set of controls is installed and they are designed to match the risk profile of a business, this does not mean that they will work properly; excellent control implementation demands a culture of conscientious examination of controls and control breaches by the entire organization. The internal audit department plays a large role here, conducting assessments of controls and issuing warnings about any deficiencies found.

Only through a continuing and company-wide focus on the importance of controls is it possible to have a robust set of controls. Thus, a top-notch control system involves both the controls themselves and the commitment of the organization behind them.

# Chapter 6
# Information Technology Auditing

## Introduction

Information technology (IT) is an essential area for the internal auditor, since it may present a business with unusually high risk levels. This is especially the case when its processes are heavily reliant on computer systems in order to function properly. An additional concern for the auditor is when users can access company IT systems from a broad array of devices, and especially when they can do so from off-site locations, making it easier for someone to gain unauthorized access to company systems. Here are several additional risk areas relating to IT:

- The selection of computer systems that are not aligned with the needs of the business
- Failed roll-outs of new computer systems
- Poorly designed software that does not function as intended
- Stored data that has been improperly validated
- Power failures that crash computer systems
- The failure of IT connections between the company and its suppliers and customers
- Confidential information being stored on off-site computers
- Loss of confidential information to third parties
- Network transmissions of data that are intercepted
- Malware attacks on company systems

In this chapter, we discuss the purpose of IT auditing, how the internal auditor can become involved in business advisory audits, audit ranking criteria, and a number of related issues.

## The Purpose of IT Auditing

The ongoing auditing of IT is an essential activity, for it identifies holes in systems that can be used to illegally extract data from a business, as well as to corrupt its systems. Locating these potential issues is critical, since plugging them could keep a business from losing its trade secrets, or from having essential systems go down. Consequently, the purpose of IT auditing involves two tasks, which are the initial identification of problems and the subsequent reporting of these findings to ensure that they are fixed. Ideally, the outcome should be not just the reporting of identified problems but also the improvement of the underlying systems.

There may be cases in which an internal audit team finds issues, but management decides not to make the recommended changes. This is still a useful function, for the auditor has identified an issue. If management decides that the cost of remediation is too high, then at least it is operating from a complete set of information. Also, the auditor now has a known problem that can be examined again at regular intervals, to see if the issue has altered – which also presents an opportunity to bring it to the attention of management again.

## Special Auditor Skills

The internal auditor needs a specialized skill set in order to understand the processes and systems under review. At a minimum, auditors involved in this area should have a deep understanding of the basic components of their company's information systems, as well as the IT risks that may impinge upon the firm's objectives. They should also understand how IT governance functions, how IT risks are being managed, and the nature of the controls that have been applied to IT. Finally, they should understand the software applications and computer hardware being used by the business units to which they have been assigned for audit engagements.

## Business Advisory Audits

A key role of the internal auditor is to act as an advisor in building robust IT systems within a business. This means taking on the role of a consultant and wading into the details of how systems work, where they have failings, and what can be done to improve them. This can be done in four ways, which are as follows:

- *Up-front involvement*. The auditor can act as an advisor in the initial construction of a system. By engaging at this stage, it is much easier and less expensive to build controls into the system that will improve its security, integrity, and/or reliability. The much more expensive alternative is to spot problems after a system has been installed, which requires an extensive effort to shoehorn the necessary controls into the system. An added advantage of advising on projects during their design stage is that the auditor gains a detailed understanding of how each system was constructed, which makes it easier to identify flaws. It may still be necessary to audit each system later, to see if the recommended controls were properly implemented.

- *Consulting audits*. The internal auditor can act as a consultant, working at the behest of department managers who want to have specific systems examined quickly and receive improvement recommendations. These engagements are designed to get the auditor in and out as quickly as possible, with reduced attention to large sample sizes or extensive documentation. Instead, the auditor only delves into a system as far as is needed to extract useful improvement suggestions for the manager requesting the work. In this case, the auditor is not expected to come back later to verify that his or her recommendations were enacted; since the manager requested the work, it is up to the manager to decide whether to take further action. Another benefit is that these engagements sometimes uncover a major problem, in which case senior management is notified and corrective actions are mandated.

- *Knowledge dispersal.* The auditor can continually push knowledge of controls out into the company. By expanding the general knowledge base about controls among employees, they will be more likely to incorporate the correct controls into their systems without the auditor needing to become actively involved in any specific systems. This can be done in several ways. For example, one might state on the department's intranet site the standard list of IT audit activities that the auditor engages in, or post a discussion of what controls should be included in specific types of IT applications. As another example, the internal auditor could post the problems found during an IT audit at another facility, which the IT staff elsewhere in the company could then use to enact improvements in their own systems. In the latter example, it may make more sense to proactively push this information out to the various IT employees, rather than just posting it to the department's intranet site and hoping that someone will read it.
- *Tool sharing.* The auditor can make available any audit software that he or she uses during audits. This usually involves making the IT managers aware of the existence of these tools and providing training in their use. There may be issues with software licensing, if many people will be using them. Nonetheless, the widespread use of audit tools by IT staff can uncover issues more quickly than when they are only used as part of an IT audit.

Of the preceding items, consulting audits are especially important, since they show the benefits of having internal auditors assist the department managers, which in turn creates greater demand for their services. When fully rolled out, they can go a long way toward improving the operations of a business. Knowledge dispersal and tool sharing tend to be less effective, since they require the active use of the provided information and tools by IT employees, which may not be forthcoming.

## Project Ranking Process

We have just discussed the types of business advisory work in which an internal auditor might engage. That still leaves the main work of the internal auditor, which is conducting IT assessments. These assessments are more formal, and involve testing, the formulation and reporting of findings, resolution plans – and documentation of every step in the process. Given the many steps (and hours) involved, the assessment process should only be directed at high-risk activities or on areas where the amount of value added is expected to be quite high. To be truly effective in targeting IT areas, the internal audit manager should rank every possible assessment project within the company, from which targeted audits are selected. This ranking process begins with a list of prospective areas that would profit from an audit investigation. The following general areas are likely sources for this project list:

- *Centralized functions*. Among the most crucial areas are those IT functions that have been centralized, since corrections made in these areas can have a broad impact on IT throughout the organization. Audits in these areas tend to focus on management of the environment. For example, one might examine change management, patch management, and security monitoring within these functions. Examples of centralized IT functions are:
  - o Central help desk
  - o Database management
  - o Firewall management
  - o Mainframe operations
  - o Mobile services
  - o Network security
  - o Server administration

- *Decentralized functions*. Other IT functions are decentralized, which means that they are managed locally. For example, PC support might be localized, rather than being managed from a central location. These functions might have been decentralized because a lower level of risk was associated with them; this may drive the prioritization of decentralized functions for audits. It can be difficult to ascertain all decentralized functions, so ask the relevant IT managers for a list of them.

- *Business applications*. Most business applications can be dealt with through a financial audit, rather than an IT audit. Nonetheless, it can make sense to evaluate each one to see if it contains any IT elements worthy of examination. This might involve an examination of the server on which an application resides or the related software change controls.

- *Strategic priorities*. Consider including on the project list any activities associated with the strategic direction of the company. Ensuring that these activities function properly minimizes the risk of failure in those areas most in need of success. For example, if the company is planning to roll out a new product line, then prioritize an examination of the functionality of the online platform through which it will be sold.

Once this list has been developed, the second step is to develop a methodology for ranking everything on the list. There are many criteria that can be included in the ranking, perhaps with weightings based on the perceived risk level associated with each one. Here are several examples of the ranking criteria that could be used:

- *Known issues*. If there are pre-existing problems in an area, this certainly warrants consideration in prioritizing audit projects.

- *Inherent risk*. An audit area may be prone to certain risks, based on prior analyses of the area, even though no risks are currently known to exist.

- *Management suggestions*. Members of the management team may request that certain areas be examined. This is not a minor ranking criterion, because those managers may have access to better information than the audit manager about where problems may exist.

- *Value added.* There may be a significant upside to the business if an area were to be targeted, perhaps in the form of recommendations for a more stream-lined process. This area is of particular interest when it is tied to the strategic direction of the company.

A possible additional ranking criterion is a rotation schedule, where certain areas are considered so critical to the business that they must be audited on a regular basis. However, this concept can be overused, where audits are assigned to certain areas simply because they are on the rotation schedule, and not because they have a high point assignment from the other ranking criteria.

An example of how the preceding ranking criteria can be used to rank potential audits appears in the following exhibit.

**Sample IT Audit Ranking**

| | | | Point Assignments | | | |
|---|---|---|---|---|---|---|
| Audit Project | Priority | Total Points | Known Issues | Inherent Risk | Management Suggestions | Value Added |
| Server administration | 1 | 20 | 4 | 8 | 2 | 6 |
| Network security | 2 | 18 | 6 | 5 | 6 | 1 |
| Firewall management | 3 | 17 | 0 | 6 | 8 | 3 |
| Database management | 4 | 15 | 2 | 2 | 5 | 6 |

When using the preceding criteria to rank audit projects, it might make sense to give some additional weighting to those areas in which there are known issues, especially if those issues carry significant risks for the business.

The number of audits that can be conducted will be limited, and depends on the amount of resources available to the internal audit manager. For example, out of a list of 35 areas, it will only be possible to conduct audits for the top 10. When this is the case, it can make sense to conduct an especially detailed comparison of the audit areas just within and outside of the cutoff line, to ensure that those areas truly requiring the most attention will be audited.

## Auditing IT Governance

The IT function frequently encapsulates a large part of the investment made in a busi-ness, both in terms of fixed assets (hardware and software) and personnel (who tend to be paid quite well). In addition to the investment made, the IT function may play a large role in corporate strategy. For both reasons, it makes sense for the internal audi-tor to pay attention to the governance structure associated with IT, to ensure that the function is being used properly. The ideal governance structure for IT is one in which stakeholders from throughout the organization have a say in IT development projects. These stakeholders can include the board of directors, senior management, and users at the departmental level. To investigate governance issues, the auditor can engage in the following activities:

- *Verify stakeholder involvement.* Assess the extent to which stakeholders need to give their approval before resource commitments are made to projects. Mandatory approval makes it more likely that projects will be examined in detail to ensure that they meet user requirements before funding is allocated to them.
- *Assess strategy linkage.* Examine the extent to which planned IT operations align with the strategic plan for the entire business. Ideally, senior management should be reviewing how much IT funding is being used to support the corporate strategy, versus the funding directed toward unrelated projects and maintenance.
- *Investigate responsiveness.* Assess how well the IT organization is responding to the issues brought up by users throughout the organization. This involves the timeliness with which changes and corrections are made, as well as the incorporation of user suggestions into forthcoming system updates.

## Auditing Entity-Level Controls

As the name implies, entity-level controls are centralized for the entire organization. If an IT process has been centralized, then it can be considered to have entity-level controls. This means that the auditor only needs to audit them once; doing so should provide a high degree of confidence that these controls have been addressed for the entire organization.

As a general rule, when a business has strong controls at the entity level, this mindset tends to trickle down through the organization, making it more likely that its other controls at the local level are also strong. This is because management has made it clear that it is deeply concerned about risks and the controls used to manage them. Conversely, when entity-level controls are not strong, the auditor should be especially watchful for IT control issues elsewhere in the company, since management has not demonstrated to the company its commitment in this area.

In the following bullet points, we describe the essential audit tests that should be conducted at the entity level:

Organization and Planning

- *Examine organizational structure.* Review the organizational structure of the IT department to see if responsibility has been specifically assigned for all key IT activities. This is needed to ensure that all activities are being performed as efficiently as possible, with minimal confusion or overlap.
- *Examine linkage to strategic plan.* Review the department's planning process to see how closely it matches the overall strategic plan of the business. Ideally, there should be a close linkage between the two, so that IT is being effective in supporting the direction in which the organization is going.

- *Examine technical planning process.* Evaluate the department's planning process to see how well it is planning for long-term technological change, including an analysis of which vendor-supported products are expected to be phased out. The planning process should clearly identify which technologies will need to be replaced, and how the company plans to do so.

## Employee Issues

- *Evaluate skill monitoring processes.* Verify that the department has sufficient processes in place to evaluate the skill level of IT employees. This should include training and periodic performance evaluations. These processes need to mandate ongoing evaluations, since skill levels will need to change, depending on the types of new technologies being installed by the company.
- *Evaluate termination procedures.* Determine the robustness of the department's procedures for shutting down system access as soon as a person leaves the employment of the company. This should include the return of company-owned equipment, such as laptops.

## Operability Issues

- *Examine user feedback loop.* Determine whether end users have the capability to report IT problems back to the department. The auditor should not just investigate the nature of the feedback process, but also whether these complaints are reviewed and acted upon in a timely manner. This may involve an examination of the department's problem and resolution tracking system.
- *Evaluate service management systems.* Review the oversight systems being used to manage any IT services that have been outsourced, such as web server hosting and PC support. This examination should include the vendor selection process, the definition of roles and responsibilities, performance monitoring, and management oversight.

## System Issues

- *Inspect system configuration controls.* Examine the department's procedures for scheduling and applying hardware and software changes to systems. These procedures should address requests for changes, risk assessments, the testing and scheduling of changes, communicating them to users, implementation, and the use of roll-backs when changes do not work.
- *Evaluate media disposal.* Examine the department's procedures for disposing of old storage media, since inadequate disposal can result in the loss of confidential data. This can include the use of encryption[1] on storage devices, or the destruction or degaussing of storage media.

---

[1] Encryption is the process of converting data into a code, to prevent unauthorized access. The sender uses an encryption algorithm to convert the original data into a code equivalent. The recipient then decodes it back into its original form.

- *Examine capacity monitoring systems.* Evaluate the department's procedures for monitoring the capacity of existing computer systems and applications and anticipating when they will need to be upgraded.

## Purchasing Issues

- *Review equipment procurement.* Review the department's asset management procedures. This means ensuring that a formal approval process is used to acquire the most expensive assets, only enough assets are acquired to meet current needs, assets are being tagged and tracked, leased equipment is returned at the end of the applicable leases, and older equipment is replaced in a timely manner.

## Legal Issues

- *Review license compliance.* Examine the department's processes for ensuring that it is in compliance with its various software licenses. This involves tracking the software being used by each employee and matching it to a database of purchased software licenses.

A concern in this area is that a centralized process does not always remain that way. The IT manager may choose to decentralize some activities, perhaps for excellent operational reasons. If so, the internal auditor will need to deal with them individually by location, using the audit techniques described in the sections later in this chapter.

## Auditing Cybersecurity Programs

Cybersecurity is the practice of protecting networks, devices, and data from unauthorized access or criminal use, as well as the practice of ensuring confidentiality, integrity, and the availability of information. Given the importance of these activities in protecting a business, one should routinely engage in auditing activities. The types of actions to pursue can vary considerably by company, depending on the type of business the organization is in and its overall size. For example, an online retail store handles the credit card information of its customers, and so needs a way to protect that information from unauthorized access. Conversely, a defense contractor wants to protect the technical details of its products, while a soft drink company wants to guard the formulas for its drinks. Given these differences, the internal auditor may only need to pursue a portion of the following audit tests:

## Organization and Planning

- *Verify responsibility.* Determine whether someone with a sufficiently high level of authority is responsible for cybersecurity, such as the chief information officer or the chief information security officer. This responsibility needs to be centralized, so that there are no cybersecurity issues for which there is no clearly identified responsible party.

- *Evaluate risk identification process.* Examine how the company identifies the risks associated with cybersecurity issues. Ideally, this should include a periodic threat assessment and third-party testing of security controls.
- *Determine program scope.* Evaluate the scope of activities of the company's cybersecurity program. This can include the development of security guidelines for the entire company, as well as activities to identify vulnerabilities and educate employees about them. The program should also engage in the collection of data about security incidents and remediate them, so that the company can upgrade its operations.

## Employee Issues

- *Evaluate security knowledge.* Assess the knowledge level of cybersecurity personnel to see if they have the requisite knowledge to perform their jobs. To do so, review job descriptions to see if they mandate the specific knowledge needed for these positions, and that the job descriptions are updated at regular intervals. Also review the training schedule for these employees, both in terms of the types of training provided and whether they have taken the classes. Finally, examine performance review documentation to see if their evaluations have been based to some degree on how current their knowledge is.
- *Review cybersecurity training.* Examine the extent to which cybersecurity training is provided to new employees. This training should include the risks to which employees will be subjected and encompass targeted security training, based on their specific job functions. Also review the frequency with which this training is repeated over time, and the processes used to ensure that the training has been completed for targeted individuals.

## Operability Issues

- *Evaluate security compliance.* Review the adequacy of the company's IT security policy, how well it is communicated to employees, whether it is monitored, and how well it is being enforced. Ideally, the policy should cover how the firm's information should be used, how it should be retained, remote connectivity rules, and the mandated security level for servers, desktops, laptops, and so forth. This examination can extend to a review of the company's password policy, which should address the password length and level of difficulty, account lockouts after a certain number of attempts, and the period of time after which passwords must be changed.
- *Evaluate incident response functions.* Assess the extent to which responses are being made to incidents. For a sufficiently major event, there should be a formal incident response process, with a documented procedure. Ideally, this procedure should address the criteria that will trigger different levels of response, who would be in charge, when to bring in other people, and guidelines for how to handle certain events.

- *Assess security policy integration.* Evaluate the extent to which the rest of the IT organization understands cybersecurity issues and integrates this awareness into their software development and system administration activities. This can include the prompt installation of software patches, as well as the use of security scanning tools during software development to spot vulnerabilities.
- *Assess security effectiveness.* Determine how the organization judges whether its security controls are effective. This step is needed because management should select only those controls that make the most sense for the organization, rather than every possible control – which is not cost-effective.

System Issues

- *Examine security monitoring.* Assess the extent to which the company has deployed resources to monitor for adverse security events. This involves the collection of log data and alerts from key systems to find events of interest, which may be handled automatically by a security information and event manager (SIEM); it collects and sorts through data from many sources, such as firewalls, antivirus systems, and authentication servers. A SIEM is also useful for subsequent investigations of events, since it can be set to store data for many months.
- *Assess data element protection.* Evaluate the framework being used to consistently assign protection to various data elements. For example, confidential information must be encrypted, while this is not necessary for public data. The intent is to spot instances in which too much protection is being assigned (which is expensive) or too little (which could lead to loss of the data or unauthorized access). This also includes an assessment of the policies for retaining data. Ideally, the policy should mandate data storage that is long enough to avoid legal, operational, and tax issues, but not so long that the company is incurring extra data storage costs.

## Auditing Data Centers

A data center is a group of networked computer servers that is used for the remote storage, processing, and/or distribution of large amounts of data. The typical data center is comprised of many racks of servers, uninterruptible power supplies, power conditioners, and high-grade heating, ventilation, and air conditioning systems. Larger organizations operate their own data centers in order to operate their computer systems in an environment with specific temperature, power, fire suppression, and security features.

Data centers face significant threats, such as flooding, fire, theft, sabotage, unusually high temperatures, the loss of power, and access to phone lines or the Internet being cut off. Any of these issues could either destroy a data center or render it inoperable from the perspective of users. Given these concerns, the auditor needs to be particularly concerned about the presence of controls in the following areas:

- *Alarm systems*. There should be alarms in place to detect problems with burglars, fire, water, chemical leaks, and power fluctuations. These alarms should provide the capability to assess issues remotely for specific alarm sensors.
- *Fire-suppression systems*. There should be a generous over-abundance of fire-suppression systems on the premises, since the large amount of electrical equipment increases the probability of fire. These systems are more likely to be gas-based, since a sprinkler system would damage the equipment in the facility.
- *HVAC*. A data center should have redundant heating, ventilation, and air conditioning systems, since the equipment it contains only works well within a narrow temperature and humidity range.
- *Physical security controls*. These controls validate anyone wanting to gain access to the premises. They may be based on some combination of an access code, a locked door, a badge, or a biometric sensor.
- *Power maintenance*. A data center usually needs to be operational at all times, which means that it may need its own power source, power conditioning to flatten out spikes and dips in the current, and battery backup systems to provide continual power in the event of a power cut-off.

Depending on the type, size, and configuration of a data center, the auditor may need to perform some portion or all of the following tests:

Organization and Planning

- *Assess capacity levels*. Examine the data center's upgrade plan to see if it has planned for a sufficient amount of additional capacity to meet projected usage loads in the near future.
- *Evaluate disaster recovery plan*. Assess the adequacy of the facility's disaster recovery plan. To do so, investigate whether it covers all parts of the data center, itemizes the steps to be taken and the order in which a recovery should be completed, and notes who is responsible for which tasks. The plan should address such additional matters as when to invoke the plan, who to contact, and where to maintain additional copies of it. The assessment should include a review the results of the latest test of the plan, along with an investigation of any issues found during the test.

Employee Issues

- *Examine security staff functions*. Assess the activities of the security staff. This is one of the more important site controls, since they are able to handle unusual events on the spot, which electronic systems are not equipped to do.
- *Assess alarm monitoring station*. Review the functions of the main alarm monitoring station to determine to what extent the various alarm systems are routed into it, and whether there is someone conducting monitoring activities at that station at all times. In addition, investigate the procedures at the station

to see if there are adequate and up-to-date instructions for how to deal with each alarm condition, and whether the staff is well-versed in these procedures.

## Operability Issues

- *Assess physical security.* Examine the surroundings of the facility to determine the probability of a breach in its physical security.
- *Assess physical access.* Determine the quality of the data center's ability to deny access to the facility. This means reviewing the robustness of doors, walls, and windows, as well as locking systems and the use of security guard patrols.
- *Evaluate environmental hazards.* Survey the area to see if the data center is subject to a variety of environmental hazards, such as flooding, lightning, earthquakes, tornadoes, extreme heat or cold, and so forth.
- *Assess access procedures.* Determine how well the facility's access procedures are functioning. Ideally, they should be consistently applied to everyone attempting to gain access. These procedures should be fully documented, stating who is allowed access, when they are allowed access, and whose approval is required for them to gain access.
- *Examine emergency response procedures.* Determine the extent to which the facility has emergency response procedures in place for all identified risks, such as fire, flooding, power loss, and physical intrusion on the premises.
- *Assess alternative data center.* If there is a backup data center to support the facility in the event of damage to the main facility, then assess the adequacy of the systems maintained at the backup facility, as well as how frequently they are updated with the latest data from the main facility.

## System Issues

- *Examine authentication systems.* Assess whether the physical authentication devices built into the access controls of the facility are adequate and are functioning properly. Also, evaluate how well the facility's authentication systems are logging access to it; ideally, the log should record the identification of each individual, the time and date of each access attempt, and whether each attempt succeeded or failed.
- *Evaluate access alarm systems.* Assess the extent to which alarm and surveillance systems are being used to prevent unauthorized access to the facility. In particular, look for dead spots in and around the facility where there is no coverage, or where the systems are not functioning properly.
- *Assess temperature and humidity controls.* Determine how well the HVAC systems are able to maintain a constant temperature and humidity level within those parts of the facility where computer equipment is stored.
- *Evaluate power conditioning.* Assess the extent to which power conditioning systems have been installed to eliminate power spikes and declines.

- *Examine battery backup systems.* Investigate whether battery backup systems are adequate to support the systems to which they are connected, that they can support sufficiently-long operating run times, and that all critical systems have backups supporting them.
- *Assess power generators.* Verify that a backup power generator is in place and functioning correctly. Also, assess whether the frequency of generator tests is sufficient, and whether the outcomes of those tests indicate that the generator is in good working order.
- *Assess fire suppression systems.* Evaluate whether the design of the building, its fire suppression system, firestops, and fire hose systems are adequate to minimize the risk of a fire spreading through the facility.
- *Evaluate fire alarms.* Determine whether heat, smoke, or flame sensors are installed in the correct locations, that they are working properly, and that they properly route warnings to the nearest fire department. Also review the alarm testing records to ensure that the alarms are being regularly tested.
- *Assess data center monitoring systems.* Examine the monitoring systems used within the data center to evaluate how well they are identifying problems with hardware, software, and network failures. Examine any monitoring logs to see how long it takes for identified problems to be addressed and remediated.
- *Evaluate system duplication.* Examine whether there is a sufficient amount of duplicate systems in cases where system downtime will have significant negative financial effects for the business.
- *Assess data backup systems.* Evaluate the facility's procedures for data backups, including backup schedules and offsite storage of backups. Also, evaluate the facility's procedures for restoring data from backups, including an observation of a backup to a test server, noting in particular any files that were not restored.

## Auditing Networking Devices

Networking devices are needed to transmit data between data storage, users, and applications. Examples of networking equipment are routers, switches, and firewalls. A router is a hardware device that routes data from a local area network to another network connection. It only allows authorized machines to connect to other computer systems, and may log the activity passing through it. A switch is less capable than a router; it is used to network multiple computers together. A switch only works the way the hardware was designed, while a router can be configured with software.

A firewall acts as a barrier between a trusted system or network and outside connections, such as the Internet. It acts as a filter, only allowing trusted data to flow through it. The choice of firewall settings involves a trade-off between convenience and security, where the system administrator has to decide whether to allow a freer flow of information or to restrict it more tightly. A firewall can be created using either hardware or software, where hardware firewalls are more commonly found in business environments.

A business might also invest in an intrusion prevention system (IPS) that uses deep packet inspection to evaluate the contents of incoming message packets, to determine whether a packet is allowed to proceed to its destination. Any packets designated as malicious are blocked and reported. An IPS works in conjunction with a firewall to minimize the amount of malicious data entering a company's computer systems.

These devices need to be properly configured when they are initially installed, and it may be necessary to adjust those settings over time, as the network is developed. The proper configuration is essential, since it can impact system security. Consequently, the network administrator should maintain and update configuration settings for all network devices.

The following audit tests can be applied to network devices:

Organization and Planning

- *Examine disaster recovery plan.* Assess whether the firm's disaster recovery plan provides for the recovery of its network devices in the event of a disaster. The plan should address how to bring back up all aspects of the network infrastructure, the order in which it should be done, and who is responsible for it.

Configuration Issues

- *Assess configuration controls.* Examine how well the network administrator is planning for and executing configuration changes to network devices. This verifies whether the administrator subscribes to all relevant security mailing lists in order to be notified of patch releases, and updates them in accordance with a standard patch updating procedure.
- *Investigate configuration backups.* Determine whether current network device configurations are fully documented and stored in a secure location, along with commentary about why certain configurations are being used.

Vulnerability Issues

- *Identify unnecessary services.* Identify any unnecessary services involving network devices and make inquiries about why these services have not been shut down. Otherwise, there may be security-related risks associated with maintaining the services.
- *Evaluate vulnerability compensations.* Determine how well the network administrator is dealing with any identified vulnerabilities in the current software version. For example, one might alter the configuration settings for a router to offset the negative effects of an identified vulnerability.

## User Access Issues

- *Review user account procedures.* Examine the procedures for creating user accounts, with a particular emphasis on whether a person should be granted access to network devices. This investigation should encompass the procedures for removing access privileges for an existing user and the events triggering the removal, perhaps due to a change in job responsibilities or the termination of their employment.

## Device Issues

- *Assess password controls.* Examine whether network devices encrypt passwords, or whether they are stored in plaintext. This can also involve a review of the minimum requirements for password complexity, as well as policies for how frequently passwords should be changed.
- *Assess wireless controls.* Determine whether any wireless network being used requires device or user authentication, and whether this authentication is based on a certificate or a password.
- *Evaluate network log-keeping.* Assess whether event logs are being maintained by the network, and what the network administrator does with them. Also, review a sample of recent alerts and the level of investigation and remediation associated with them.
- *Investigate switch access.* In cases where switches are not in a secure location, verify that they require a password for user access.
- *Assess physical access.* Examine the level of physical security associated with all network equipment. This can include a review of those individuals currently allowed access, to see if this is justified, as well as whether any network equipment is located outside of the secure area.
- *Investigate network access control.* Assess the extent to which network access control is being used. Ideally, it should be used to authenticate every device and user attempting to gain access to the system, as well as whether the device is compliant with the company's latest antivirus protection. This is especially important when devices are being used to gain remote access to the network.
- *Evaluate unused interfaces.* If switches have unused ports, assess the extent to which they have been disabled. Doing so prevents intruders from using those ports to communicate with the network. Similarly, if routers have inactive interfaces, such as an Ethernet interface, they should be shut down in order to prevent unauthorized access through them.
- *Assess firewall controls.* A key evaluation point is whether the firewall denies all data packets by default. This means that data packets are only accepted when they are coming from or headed to explicitly defined addresses and ports. In addition, assess the extent to which the firewall rules are being managed to maintain a high degree of security. Also, determine whether intrusion detection systems are being used, and how frequently the underlying detection rules are reviewed and updated.

## Auditing Databases

A database is a data structure that stores organized information. In many organizations, the data stored in a database is an organization's most valuable asset, so it makes sense for the internal auditor to explore the controls associated with it.

The typical database is located behind the outer walls of the corporate IT castle, and so is not subjected to the attacks experienced every day by a firewall or web server. This tends to lead the IT staff into a false sense of complacency, where they do not think about imposing database controls. This can result in massive data breaches when an attacker manages to penetrate as far as the corporate database. Consequently, an IT audit in this area is well worth the effort. The following audit tests can be applied to a database:

Organization and Planning

- *Examine capacity management.* Gauge how well the capacity of the database is being monitored in relation to projected needs. The database administrator should have a capacity expansion plan that is triggered when certain capacity usage thresholds are exceeded.

Configuration Issues

- *Evaluate database version.* Determine whether the database is the most recent version. If not, see if the version is still being supported by the vendor. If not, patch updates are no longer being supplied, which can cause control issues. Also, if the database *is* being supported, verify that the latest patches have been installed, or that the latest patches are being reviewed prior to being installed.

Vulnerability Issues

- *Assess database monitoring.* Evaluate whether the database is being monitored for unusual activity, with follow-up when this is the case. This monitoring can encompass reviews of who is accessing the system, what changes were made to it, and traffic levels.

User Access Issues

- *Assess access restrictions.* Determine whether access to the database is restricted to the system administrator. Users should not be able to connect to the database directly; they should only be able to do so through an application.
- *Examine directory permissions.* Evaluate the level of access being given to the directory on which the database is installed. This should be tightly locked down, since improper access to this directory can result in database files being corrupted.
- *Evaluate account creations.* Determine whether the procedures used to create user accounts are sufficiently restrictive. Accounts should only be created

when there is a clear business reason for doing so, and when the event has been approved.

- *Gauge password difficulty*. Evaluate the difficulty of passwords, including minimum required lengths and compositions, password aging, password lockouts, and so forth. Also conduct a search for easily guessed passwords.
- *Search for default access codes*. Conduct a search for default user IDs and passwords. Also, review the database administrator's procedure for forcing these defaults to be changed when an account is first used.

Encryption Issues

- *Evaluate database encryption*. Data should be encrypted where it is stored within the database, especially since the database may be backup up to another location that is less secure, and where the data can be accessed. Review a sample of the data to ensure that this is the case.
- *Evaluate network encryption*. Data should be encrypted as it moves across the network, since the network is not a secure environment. Conduct a sample of network traffic to ensure that this is the case.

## Auditing Storage

Data storage platforms have traditionally been maintained within an organization, possibly at multiple locations within a network, from which data can be shared across it, as needed. Storage can also be located in the cloud, typically in a data center operated by a third party, from which it is accessed by a company's applications as needed. The following audit steps can be applied to data storage:

- *Assess capacity management*. Evaluate the processes used to monitor the usage of storage capacity, and how that is expected to change as part of the company's current short-term and medium-term plans.
- *Evaluate data backup*. Assess how well the company's data backup procedures operate.
- *Evaluate encryption*. The same audit steps can be conducted for data storage as those already noted for the auditing of databases.
- *Review patch updates*. Determine whether the IT staff has access to information about patch updates for the storage infrastructure, and is actively installing them.

A business can address most of the preceding storage issues by formulating and continually updating a capacity management plan, since the issues noted here can generally be remediated by making investments in the storage infrastructure.

## Auditing End-User Computing Devices

A large proportion of the computing activity within a business is conducted on the personal desktop and laptop computers of its employees. It is generally more difficult to impose sufficient controls on these devices, which means that they are an ideal access point for an attacker who wants to gain access to a company's systems. There are multiple auditing steps for the internal auditor to pursue in this area, which are documented in the following bullet points:

Organization and Planning

- *Assess device policies.* Evaluate how the company's IT policies address the use of personally-owned devices on company business. It should state the circumstances under which they can be used and how they are to be kept secure. The policy should clarify those circumstances under which it is not acceptable to conduct business on such a device, as well as what types of data can and cannot be stored on it.

Configuration Issues

- *Review at-risk devices.* Evaluate which devices are at greatest risk of being stolen, and examine the types of data stored on them.
- *Examine backup system.* Determine how well the company has implemented a system of data backups on end-user computing devices.
- *Investigate encryption levels.* Review whether end-user computing devices contain fully encrypted data storage.
- *Review for unlicensed software.* Assess the company's process for procuring software licenses for employees, as well as its process for verifying that only authorized software copies are stored on end-user computing devices.

User Access Issues

- *Gauge user rights.* The rights granted to someone operating an end-user computing device should be as restrictive as possible, to minimize the risk of having an unauthorized intruder gain broad access to company systems through it. This means discussing user rights with the IT manager and verifying that actual user rights granted match what the manager stated.
- *Search for default accounts.* One of the easiest ways for an intruder to gain access to the company system is to access a default account on an end-user device. Consequently, one should assess the extent to which default accounts are still present on these devices.
- *Evaluate passwords.* Every end-user computing device should have a password. Accordingly, review the strength of the controls on passwords, such as password complexity, aging, and length.
- *Gauge access granting process.* Evaluate the procedures used to grant user access to company systems.

Oversight Issues

- *Evaluate auditee support personnel.* In a widely distributed environment, support personnel need access to employee devices that may be off-premises. Since the support personnel will need to gain access to those devices as part of their support activities, the auditor should examine the policies granting system access to the support personnel. Ideally, support personnel should not have access to the user IDs or passwords of employees.
- *Evaluate ticketing system.* Gauge how well the customer service function of the IT department is managing the employee support function as it relates to end-user computing devices. This usually involves the recordation of each employee contact on a service ticket record, which is then tracked until the associated issue has been resolved.

## Auditing Applications

An application is a software program that runs on a computer. Examples of applications are an accounting system, a warehouse management system, and a production scheduling system. Each of these applications was developed separately, probably by a separate vendor, and so has different control issues associated with it. Given these differences, it can be difficult to develop a universal set of auditing activities to apply to them. Nonetheless, the following auditor actions are more likely to be required for most applications:

Organization and Planning

- *Gauge application support.* Evaluate whether there is a problem tracking and resolution system for the software, and how well it works. Also, assess the usability of system documentation and training in assisting application users, as well as the functionality of any help desk function.

Configuration Issues

- *Examine data input controls.* Assess the extent to which an application incorporates validation controls to ensure that the data input into it has a high degree of integrity.
- *Assess audit trails.* Evaluate the extent to which the application generates an audit trail that can be used to track down anomalies. The audit trail should store data about what changes were made, who made them, and when the changes were made.
- *Verify backup processes.* Determine how well the application is backed up. This includes the frequency of backups, what is backed up (both data and the application itself), and whether the backups are stored off-site in a secure location. Also, test whether the recovery function from backup works properly; there should be a recovery procedure that identifies all steps to be conducted, as well as who is responsible for it.

- *Assess data retention.* Determine how long data is retained in the system, and whether that retention period accords with the business and legal requirements of the organization.

## Vulnerability Issues

- *Investigate security monitoring.* Determine the extent to which the application has processes in place to scan for vulnerabilities, as well as to generate alerts when unusual transactions occur. In addition, assess whether any issues highlighted by this monitoring are being investigated and remediated.
- *Review software change controls.* Gauge the functionality of the company's controls relating to changes made to application software. Ideally, software developers should be forced to have all software changes reviewed, tested, and approved before they are allowed into production.

## User Access Issues

- *Evaluate administrator function.* Determine whether there is an administrator function for the application, and whether it is configured to add, delete, and modify user access to the application.
- *Examine authentication system.* Assess how well the application authenticates each user, typically with a user ID and password scheme.
- *Review access levels.* Gauge the extent to which the application gives varying levels of access to users. Also, evaluate the process for deciding which person is assigned the various access levels.
- *Assess access removal procedure.* Determine whether a procedure exists for removing access to the application, how well it works, and whether it is consistently followed.
- *Review default passwords.* Assess whether any default passwords are still in use. Further, check the application settings to see if they require a user to change a default password when the person first accesses the application.
- *Verify log-off criteria.* Ascertain whether there is an automatic log-off function that is triggered when an application has not been used for a certain period of time.

## Encryption Issues

- *Assess encryption usage.* Determine whether encryption is being used by the application to protect the data stored within it.

## Auditing Outsourced Operations

Many computer applications are outsourced, because it can be less expensive to do so. A company commonly finds that it can avoid the substantial up-front purchase costs of hardware and software, instead substituting a monthly usage fee that varies based on the number of users and usage levels. In some cases, a company will have a vendor run its own data centers, on the theory that the vendor has better expertise in the IT area, allowing management to concentrate on the core competencies of the business. Other areas that are commonly outsourced are help desk support and PC support.

A variation on the outsourcing concept is cloud computing, which is the practice of using a network of remote servers hosted on the Internet to store, manage, and process data, rather than doing so on a local server or personal computer. In the case of cloud computing, management does not have to concern itself with any of the back-end infrastructure associated with its computing operations, and lowers its costs by sharing computing resources with other customers of the applicable cloud computing provider. In essence, a business uses cloud computing to acquire IT resources from vendors on demand, and only as needed, so that the service level needed can expand or contract as required.

The internal auditor would have a difficult time conducting audit reviews of IT vendors, since they are generally located off-site and also are under different management. Fortunately, this problem is addressed by SSAE 18, which was developed by the American Institute of Certified Public Accountants to deal with service organizations. This audit standard allows a service organization to demonstrate the effectiveness of its own system of controls, rather than having each customer's auditors conduct their own audit procedures on its operations. This means that the vendor hires an outside auditor (the service auditor) to conduct an audit on its controls, after which that auditor issues a report attesting to the effectiveness of those controls. A company's auditor can then request a copy of this report.

A *type 1 report* is management's description of a service organization's system and a service auditor's report on that description and on the suitability of the design of controls. A *type 2* report is management's description of a service organization's system and a service auditor's report on that description and on the suitability of the design and operating effectiveness of controls. Both reports can assist the auditor in identifying and assessing the risk of control failures, but a type 1 report does not provide evidence concerning the operating effectiveness of controls. A type 2 report may offer little audit evidence when there is minimal overlap between the period covered by the report and the period being audited. When using one of these reports, the auditor should evaluate whether the report covers the appropriate period, and whether it provides sufficient and appropriate evidence for understanding the vendor's internal controls.

In short, it can be quite useful to rely on the work of others when auditing outsourced functions, if they are independent of the vendor, conduct their work objectively, and are knowledgeable in the reviewed areas. By relying on this work, the internal auditor may be able to significantly scale back on his or her own activities.

The auditor should address the following topics when engaged in an audit of out-sourced operations:

Organization and Planning

- *Examine disaster recovery plan.* Review the vendor's disaster recovery plan to ascertain how well it is prepared to recover from a disaster at its facilities.
- *Evaluate software license compliance.* Review the company's software agreements to ensure that it is in compliance with their terms when it shifts the hosting of its acquired software to a vendor.

Configuration Issues

- *Evaluate data segregation.* Assess how well the company's data is being segregated from that of the vendor's other customers.

Vulnerability Issues

- *Assess vendor access to company data.* Investigate the controls placed by the vendor over its employees' access to company data.
- *Examine notification rights.* Evaluate the company's documented right to be notified if the vendor suffers a security breach.

User Access Issues

- *Evaluate identity management.* Assess how the vendor handles identity management. This ranges from the required complexity and aging of passwords to the use of multifactor authentication. Ideally, the vendor's controls should be at least as robust as those of the company.

Encryption Issues

- *Evaluate encryption.* Evaluate the level of data encryption being used by the vendor. This is especially important when company data is being commingled with the data of the vendor's other customers.

Oversight Issues

- *Inspect vendor contract.* Determine from the vendor contract how the vendor's performance will be measured, and the exact structure of those measurements. They typically include expected uptime, problem response time, and issue resolution time. Also look for a right-to-audit clause, which allows the auditor to conduct audit work pertaining to vendor operations.
- *Obtain SSAE report.* Request a copy of the vendor's SSAE 18 report and peruse it to see if there are any control-related issues, as well as the vendor's remediation plans for them.
- *Investigate vendor oversight.* Evaluate the company's processes for overseeing the operations of the vendor. This usually involves comparing actual

performance to the metrics laid out in the vendor contract, presenting problems to the vendor, and monitoring the vendor's remediation efforts.

- *Gauge data retention practices.* Determine whether the vendor retains data using the same policies imposed by the company.
- *Evaluate vendor staffing methods.* Assess the vendor's processes for maintaining a sufficiently high level of staff quality for those personnel working on company-related operations.
- *Review assets.* If any company assets have been placed under the control of the vendor, the auditor can review them periodically and assess their condition.
- *Investigate regulatory issues.* The process that has been outsourced may be subject to government regulation. When this is the case, examine the process to ensure that the vendor is conducting it in accordance with the mandates of the applicable government entity.

In short, outsourcing of selected functions is fairly common in the IT area, but it can bring up a number of issues for the internal auditor to investigate.

## Summary

The sheer volume of audit activities noted in this book should make it clear that IT auditing can be an overwhelming endeavor, especially in a larger organization that has many locations and interlinked systems. The internal auditor will need to focus on two issues in particular in order to deal with this work load. The first is having a clear prioritization process for deciding which areas will be audited and (more importantly) which ones will *not* be audited. And second, once a clearly-defined audit schedule has been produced, the internal auditor will need to assess the resources needed in order to complete that schedule by the designated dates – and convince management to provide the necessary funding. It is nearly impossible to conduct a comprehensive IT audit, so by focusing on these two issues, one can have a reasonable chance of addressing just the most essential, high-risk activities within a company's IT function.

# Chapter 7
# Fraud Prevention and Detection

## Introduction

Fraud is pervasive in many parts of the world, and exists even in those areas where people are generally considered to maintain high ethical standards. The amount of losses that businesses suffer from fraud is not minor, with many estimates exceeding 5% of sales. Given the prevalence of fraud and its inordinate cost, any business person should be deeply concerned with how fraud can be detected and prevented. When fraud can be curtailed, a business may experience profits that its competitors cannot match, thereby giving it a long-term financial advantage.

In this chapter, we discuss the nature of fraud, what causes it, fraud indicators, and how to establish a system of fraud prevention and detection.

> **Related Podcast Episodes:** Episodes 34, 215, 216, 217, 239, 245, 247, and 260 of the Accounting Best Practices Podcast discuss fraud deterrence and a variety of fraud schemes. They are available at: **accountingtools.com/podcasts** or **iTunes**

## What is Fraud?

Fraud is a false representation of the facts, resulting in the object of the fraud receiving an injury by acting upon the misrepresented facts. Fraud is proven in court by showing that the actions of an individual involved the following elements:

- A false statement of a material fact;
- Knowledge that the statement was untrue;
- Intent by the individual to deceive the victim;
- Reliance by the victim on the statement; and
- Injury sustained by the victim as a result of the preceding actions.

The key element in the preceding definition is *intent*. A company could make false representations in its financial statements simply because the accounting staff made a mistake in compiling certain financial information. This is not fraud (though it may be incompetence), since there was no intent to misstate the financial statements. Conversely, if a controller intentionally reduces the bad debt reserve in order to increase profits and thereby triggers a bonus for the management team, this *is* fraud, because a false statement was intentionally made.

For the purposes of this chapter, we are adding to the definition of fraud any type of theft from a business. Doing so expands the number of crimes enormously. For example, the theft of funds before they are recorded (skimming) and the theft of assets from a business (larceny) can now be considered fraud. These additional crimes do not fall within the classic definition of fraud. However, the detection and prevention of these activities involve actions that are quite similar to those used for "classic" fraudulent activities. By including additional types of crime, we are providing the reader with a broader knowledge of activities to guard against.

## Fraud Triggers

Under what conditions does someone commit fraud? There are three interlocking conditions, known as the *fraud triangle*, under which fraud is most likely to flourish. These conditions are:

- *Perceived pressure.* A person may be liable for significant liabilities, such as the cost of supporting sick relatives, college loans, car loans, and so forth. Or, they may have an expensive habit that requires ongoing funding. When the individual sees no way out of the situation, they may resort to fraud. However, there may only be a *perceived* level of pressure, such as earning comparatively less than one's friends. This latter situation can trigger expectations for a better lifestyle, perhaps involving a sports car, foreign travel, or a larger house. When a person does not see a clear path to meeting these expectations by honest means, he or she may resort to dishonest alternatives.
- *Opportunity.* When the preceding pressures are present, a person must also see an opportunity to commit fraud. For example, a maintenance worker may realize that there are no controls over checking out and returning tools; this is an opportunity for theft.
- *Rationalization.* An additional issue that is needed for fraud to continue over a period of time is the ability of the perpetrator to rationalize the situation as being acceptable. For example, a person stealing from a company's petty cash box might rationalize it as merely borrowing, with the intent of paying back the funds at a later date. As another example, a management team adjusts reported earnings for a few months during mid-year, in the expectation that sales will rise towards the end of the year, allowing them to eliminate the adjustments by year-end.

The issues noted here tend to interact. For example, if a person is under an intense amount of financial pressure and there is a serious opportunity for fraud, then the level of rationalization needed to justify committing fraud will be quite low. Conversely, if there is little pressure and only a modest opportunity to do so, then it will take a much higher level of rationalization to justify the fraud. Consequently, a good approach to proactively dealing with fraud is to work on all of these areas – reducing the financial pressure on employees and minimizing the number and size of opportunities for fraud.

We cover the pressure, opportunity, and rationalization issues in more detail in the following sub-sections.

## Perceived Pressure

The most obvious type of pressure that may impact a person is financial pressure. While one might associate real financial pressure with someone living in a car or under a bridge, anyone can have a perceived amount of financial pressure even when they already earn a substantial amount of money. Consider the following situations:

- A person is living well beyond his means. For example, a production worker loves sports cars and is determined to have one, even though his hourly wage does not begin to qualify him for a car loan. Or, a corporate executive wants a private jet, so he will misrepresent his company's profits in order to sell shares at a higher price and then buy the jet.
- A person has incurred a large amount of debt. His current wage might have been sufficient under all normal circumstances, but the additional amount of debt payments renders his situation much less tenable. The same situation arises when a person's wages are being garnished.
- A person is suddenly confronted with a large expenditure. For example, a person's spouse is uninsured, and she must now undergo expensive radiation therapy to treat cancer.
- A person wants to be perceived as being successful. This calls for the acquisition of a large home, a cabin in the country, a fishing boat, and other toys. This person is more concerned with the image being conveyed than having a low level of integrity.

Financial pressure can extend to the management team when they are trying to protect the viability of the company. For example, an entity's financial results have been gradually declining, and it is in danger of breaching its loan covenants, which will trigger a loan call by the bank. To avoid this situation, the management team adjusts the financial statements to keep the entity's reported results just higher than the thresholds stated in the loan covenants.

A type of behavior that can cause financial problems is any type of vice. For example, a person may be unable to stop gambling, and racks up enormous gambling debts. Or, an individual is addicted to hard drugs, and is always in need of cash to fund the habit. As another example, a person has a mistress and needs to support her lifestyle.

A different type of pressure is the desire to get even with an employer. For example, a person might have been denied a promotion, and so elects to commit fraud in order to make the employer "pay" for this decision. A person might feel the same way if he perceives his compensation to be unusually low, or if his contributions to the business have not been acknowledged.

Yet another type of pressure comes from the employer. This pressure usually comes in the form of a performance standard that must be met. For example, the senior management team imposes a very difficult commission plan on the sales staff; to meet their targets, the sales staff needs to sell more to customers than they really need. Similarly, if a very high profit goal has been set, the accounting staff feels that it needs to use subterfuge, such as keeping the books open into the following month in order to record additional sales.

## Opportunity

A key factor contributing to fraud is the presence of a perceived opportunity to steal assets. These opportunities can come in many shapes and sizes. The opportunity for fraud is certainly enhanced when the environment within an organization is permissive, as would be the case in the following situations:

- *Absence of controls*. A key control might be missing that would otherwise prevent a theft from occurring, or at least detect it after the fact. This situation is more likely to arise when new systems are installed or existing ones are modified without paying attention to the underlying controls. In addition, a business that is not audited is less likely to have an independent review of its system of controls, and so may have no idea that it is lacking a key control. When any of the following types of controls are missing, it represents an opportunity for fraud to occur:
    - o The presence of authorizations for transactions, so that a manager must issue an approval before a transaction can be completed, or employees are only authorized to engage in transactions up to a certain dollar limit.
    - o Segregation of duties, so that it would require more than one person to commit fraud.
    - o Independent reviews of a person's work, perhaps involving job rotations or supervisory reviews, so that a person could not keep up a fraud for a long period of time.
    - o Controls over physical access to assets, so that someone would need to break into a controlled area in order to steal assets.
    - o Proper supporting documentation for records, to identify the nature of a transaction and any related authorizations.
- *Accountability*. The level of accountability for all tasks should be quite clear within a business. When this is not the case, controls are significantly weaker, since no one is required to engage in preventive or detective activities.
- *Internal audit*. When there is an active internal audit department that is visibly examining transactions, this presents a significant deterrent. When there is no such group within a business, employees are more likely to engage in fraud, since there is no one in an oversight role.
- *Transitions*. Whenever there are layoffs, spin-offs, mergers, and plant closures, there is an increased risk that the control environment will break down, frequently because the key employees with a deep knowledge of controls are no longer working for the company.
- *Management example*. There may be a general environment of permissiveness within an organization. For example, if the management team is known to "play loose" with their expense reports, employees are more likely to

follow their example. Or, if management is known to be creating fictitious customers in order to increase the reported sales level, employees will be more tempted to cheat the company and its investors in other ways. In this environment, the effectiveness of even a strong set of controls is weakened, since employees are more likely to work together to defeat the control system.

- *Management communication.* Ideally, management should be communicating constantly with employees regarding acceptable behavior, using training, a code of conduct, and other tools. If these communications are not present, employees do not have a clear indication of what is right and wrong, and so will be more inclined to step over the line and commit fraud.
- *Work environment.* In a negative work environment, employees have a vastly lower association with the business, and so are more likely to engage in fraudulent activities. Situations that can contribute to a negative work environment are:
  - A persistently high level of negative feedback from management
  - A strongly hierarchical management structure, where consideration is rarely given to suggestions from people lower in the organization
  - A widespread sense of job inequity, such as advancement being given to a small group of favored employees
  - Extremely difficult performance targets that are rarely attained
  - Minimal acknowledgement of good employee performance
  - Unusually low compensation and benefit packages

- *Vetting practices.* The human resources department must spend the time to research the backgrounds of all job candidates prior to hiring them. Otherwise, people with criminal backgrounds, questionable performances at prior employers, or falsified resumes will be hired, which leads to a higher incidence of fraud.

## Rationalization

Someone committing fraud almost always needs to have some way to rationalize this conduct. There are many possible rationalizations, such as:

- I am taking the money from a corrupt organization
- I am using the money to help others
- The organization should have paid me this money
- This is only borrowing for a short time, and I will pay it back
- We will correct the books once we get through this rough patch and sales increase
- I have already paid enough income taxes
- If I pay more income taxes, the government will waste it anyways

With these kinds of rationalizations, a person can lie to himself that there is a good reason for engaging in fraud.

# Types of Fraud

There are a number of types of fraud that a business can experience. At the highest level, they can be broken down into two general categories, which are fraud committed *on behalf of* the organization and fraud committed *against* the organization. In the first case, employees alter the reported financial results of the business in order to make it look better than is really the case. This could be done in order to bolster the stock price, earn bonuses, or avoid a loan default. The benefit to the perpetrator may be indirect. In the latter case, employees are directly stealing from the organization, so they experience a direct benefit. Within these two classifications are a number of fraud types, which we describe in the following sub-sections.

## Financial Statement Fraud

In financial statement fraud, the management team alters the financial statements in order to reveal more sales, better profits, a more robust financial position, and/or better cash flows than is really the case. The victims of this fraud are investors and creditors. Investors are relying on the financial statements to judge the prices at which to buy or sell a company's shares, and so could make incorrect investment decisions. Creditors are relying on the statements to determine whether to loan funds or extend credit to the company, and could potentially lose these funds if the company turns out to be a poor credit risk.

## Embezzlement

When embezzlement occurs, employees either directly take assets from the company for their own use, or assist in diverting assets from the company. For example, a warehouse person could walk out with finished goods inventory, a maintenance staffer could steal tools, and a sales clerk could steal cash from the cash register. When a person assists in diverting assets, this involves taking bribes or kickbacks from outsiders who are engaged in fraudulent activities. For example:

- *Supplier kickback.* A purchasing department employee accepts a 5% kickback from a supplier in exchange for approving its bid in a competitive bidding situation. The supplier bids at a higher price than would normally be accepted, so the company is losing funds as a result of the situation.
- *Supplier bribery.* A supplier bribes the receiving manager to overlook low-quality raw materials being delivered to the company. The company suffers from a higher failure rate in its production processes as a result of using the low-quality materials.

The level of embezzlement depends on the position occupied by the perpetrator, with more senior positions having a greater ability to embezzle. It is also possible that a person with a less-senior position can also embezzle a significant amount if they take advantage of a control weakness.

**Supplier Fraud**

There are a number of ways in which a supplier can commit fraud against a company. Consider the following possibilities:

- *Bid rigging.* In a competitive bidding situation, several suppliers could collude to not bid excessively low prices, thereby keeping the company from reaping the gains normally experienced in this situation.
- *Overbilling.* A supplier could agree to one price, and then bill a higher price. This may not be obvious when the billing is obfuscated with many smaller or add-on charges. This is a particular concern in cost-plus billing arrangements where suppliers can bill the costs they have incurred; they may overload these billings with unrelated expenses.
- *Lower quality goods.* A supplier could ship lower-quality goods. This is especially hard to detect when the lower-quality items are mixed in with higher-quality goods or are integrated into completed components.
- *Short ship goods.* A supplier may slightly under-ship the number of goods ordered, and bill for the full amount. This is most common when the number of units ordered is extremely large, and it is difficult for the receiving department to affirm the exact amount received.

These issues can occur when there is not a sufficient level of oversight of the purchasing process or the receiving department. The level of fraud can be more pronounced when a supplier is bribing an employee to overlook the overbillings and other issues. This type of fraud can be subtle and unusually hard to detect when suppliers only engage in it at a very low level.

**Customer Fraud**

Customer fraud occurs when a customer refuses to pay the company or pays too little with no justification, or demands more goods or services in exchange for the amount paid. This situation most commonly arises when a customer has a significant amount of power over a company, typically because it represents a large part of the company's revenues.

A variation on the concept is for a person to impersonate a customer. For example, a bank could be persuaded to issue a bank check to a person who has misrepresented himself as being a wealthy client.

## Common Fraud Risk Indicators

There are a number of factors that make it more likely that fraud will occur or is occurring in a business. These fraud risk factors include the following:

Nature of Items

- *Size and value*. If items that can be stolen are of high value in proportion to their size (such as diamonds), it is less risky to remove them from the premises. This is a particularly critical item if it is easy for employees to do so.
- *Ease of resale*. If there is a ready market for the resale of stolen goods (such as for most types of consumer electronics), this presents an increased temptation to engage in fraud.
- *Cash*. If there is a large amount of bills and coins on hand, or cash in bank accounts, there is a very high risk of fraud. At a local level, a large balance in a petty cash box presents a considerable temptation.

Nature of Control Environment

- *Separation of duties*. The risk of fraud declines dramatically if multiple employees are involved in different phases of a transaction, since fraud requires the collusion of at least two people. Thus, poorly-defined job descriptions and approval processes present a clear opportunity for fraud.
- *Safeguards*. When assets are physically protected, they are much less likely to be stolen. This can involve fencing around the inventory storage area, a locked bin for maintenance supplies and tools, security guard stations, an employee badge system, and similar solutions. A lack of these safeguards encourages thieves.
- *Documentation*. When there is no physical or electronic record of a transaction, employees can be reasonably assured of not being caught, and so are more inclined to engage in fraud. This is also the case if there *is* documentation, but the records can be easily modified.
- *Time off*. When a business requires its employees to take the full amount of allocated time off, this keeps them from continuing to hide ongoing cases of fraud, and so is a natural deterrent. Thus, *not* having a time off policy is a fraud risk factor.
- *Related party transactions*. When there are numerous transactions with related parties, it is more likely that purchases and sales will be made at amounts that differ considerably from the market rate.
- *Complexity*. When the nature of a company's business involves very complex transactions, and especially ones involving estimates, it is easier for employees to manipulate the results of these transactions to report better results than is really the case.
- *Dominance*. When a single individual is in a position to dominate the decisions of the management team, and especially when the board of directors is weak, this individual is more likely to engage in unsuitable behavior.

- *Turnover*. When there is a high level of turnover among the management team and among employees in general, the institutional memory regarding how transactions are processed is weakened, resulting in less attention to controls.
- *Auditing*. When there is no internal audit function, it is unlikely that incorrect or inappropriate transactions will be spotted or corrected.

Pressures

- *Level of dissatisfaction*. If the work force is unhappy with the company, they will be more inclined to engage in fraud. Examples of such situations are when a layoff is imminent, benefits have been reduced, bonuses have been eliminated, promotions have been voided, and so forth.
- *Expectations*. When there is pressure from outside investors to report certain financial results, or by management to meet certain performance targets (perhaps to earn bonuses), or to meet balance sheet goals to qualify for debt financing, there is a high risk of financial reporting fraud.
- *Guarantees*. When the owners or members of management have guaranteed company debt, there will be strong pressure to report certain financial results in order to avoid triggering the guarantees.

## Fraud Prevention Activities

There are a number of ways in which to prevent fraud from being committed within an organization. In the following sub-sections, we describe a variety of approaches that include reducing the financial pressure on employees, communicating behavioral expectations to them, and maintaining a proper environment in the office.

### Combat Perceived Pressure

A business can pay a third party to manage an employee assistance program (EAP). An EAP is designed to help employees deal with a number of issues, including substance abuse and other types of addictions, money management problems, health issues, and family-related concerns. When used by a sufficient number of employees, this service can have quite a positive impact.

Another program that can reduce certain types of perceived pressure is a corporate wellness program. This program focuses on the physical health of employees, offering dietary counseling, gym memberships, and incentives to maintain a healthy lifestyle. Such a program can mitigate the risk of incurring unexpected medical bills, and relieves stress in general by promoting a healthier lifestyle.

Another way to combat perceived pressure is to actively encourage an open door policy. When employees are willing to discuss their personal problems with management, they bring up personal issues, which can then be talked about and perhaps resolved. For example, if an employee is having trouble paying for an unexpected medical bill, the company may be able to arrange for financing that will cover his immediate need, thereby mitigating perceived pressure that might otherwise result in a fraud situation.

## Hire Correctly

Part of the hiring process must be a detailed background check on all employees, to weed out those that have a history of less than ethical behavior. Certain individuals have a higher need for cash and so are more likely to steal – for example, those with drug, overspending, and gambling habits. These individuals should not be hired. Further, examine *all* of the information on a submitted resume. If any of this information proves to be false or exaggerated, do not hire the applicant. A resume and background check can be time-consuming, since some sources may not be willing to divulge information. Nonetheless, the human resources staff should be persistent in investigating these issues, rather than approving a job applicant once a certain minimum effort has been made. When supporting information is difficult to obtain, a possible reason is that the applicant is trying to hide the information.

## Communicate Expectations

The management team must create a set of the values that it wants to instill in employees, and thoroughly communicate the resulting code of conduct to employees. A code of conduct can be quite massive, but then suffers from being unreadable. A better approach is to compress the code into a short, readable document that expresses core values, and which may have addendums that expand on the basic concepts.

Discussions concerning the code of conduct, expectations for employees, and fraud-related training can be included in the introductory training program for new employees. The level of information provided concerning fraud detection may vary by the type of position. For example, a new warehouse employee might receive training on fraud detection related to the theft of inventory, while a new finance employee might instead receive fraud training targeted at cash transfers. A more detailed level of training may be provided for new members of the management team and anyone in the internal audit department. Additional topics assigned to these people may include contract and procurement fraud, bribery in international transactions, evidence of cash skimming, inventory theft detection tools, and so forth.

The communication of expectations regarding fraud should not end with the hiring process for new employees. Instead, this information should be periodically included in other communications to employees, such as the annual edition of the employee manual. Another option is to periodically run an anti-fraud campaign, using discussions, videos, and posters to bring the issue to the attention of employees.

## Provide an Example

The entire management team must set an example for the organization by always taking the most ethically correct course. Any members of management who deviate from this strict standard must be disciplined and/or fired. Otherwise, employees will see a permissive environment in the management ranks, and mimic that environment when engaged in their own activities.

The management team should also have high expectations for the ethical performance of everyone in the organization. By regularly communicating these expectations through their words and actions, managers set a high performance standard that they expect will be met.

## Establish the Work Environment

A work environment in which employees feel a strong sense of buy-in to the mission of the organization is ideal for preventing fraud, since they are not likely to steal from an organization that they support.

A sense of buy-in to a business can be particularly strong when management commits to a minimal level of employee turnover and couples it with a reasonable and fair compensation structure. In this environment, the key concerns of employees have been met, so there is no reason for them to engage in fraud. Additional adjustments to the work environment that can also reduce the incidence of fraud are:

- *Broad-based management.* The management team routinely asks employees for input on a variety of topics, which may include tactical and even strategic decisions. This likely means that the organization has a relatively flat management structure, with few levels of management. By doing so, employees have a better sense of contributing to the organization, and so are less likely to steal from it.
- *Employee interactions.* When there are issues, these items are addressed at once and openly, rather than being repressed. By doing so, it is more difficult for problems to fester, which could cause someone to "take it out" on the company by stealing from it.
- *Fair promotion criteria.* The company promotes based on the performance and abilities of its employees, rather than cronyism. When employees understand that they will be fairly considered for promotions, it is less likely that they will feel aggrieved if someone else is given a plum assignment or promotion.
- *Long-range planning.* The company focuses the attention of its employees on attaining long-term goals. Conversely, it does not force them to achieve short-term goals (such as quarterly sales figures) which are more likely to spawn a culture of financial statement fraud in order to meet those goals.
- *Performance recognition.* The company routinely recognizes a job well done. This may involve public recognition, perhaps coupled with a system of minor rewards. This activity nullifies any feelings that might fester when a person believes she has made a good effort and yet has not been recognized for it.
- *Positive feedback system.* The feedback system used by the organization emphasizes giving positive feedback to encourage employees to engage in certain types of behavior, rather than employing negative feedback to punish employees if they do not follow the mandates of management. The use of negative feedback tends to set employees against the company, making them much more open to the possibility of committing fraud.

**Handle Fraud Situations Correctly**

One way to prevent the occurrence of fraud is to always prosecute someone who is found to have committed fraud. Other employees see how the company reacts to being defrauded. When a perpetrator is pursued vigorously in court, employees will understand that there is a greatly reduced opportunity for fraud within the company, and so will be less inclined to engage in it. Further, when the company pursues restitution for the amounts stolen, this reduces the perceived gain that others might see from engaging in fraud.

In addition, there should be a highly visible process for examining and evaluating the circumstances of each fraud (likely involving the internal audit department), with corrective action to reduce the risk of fraud occurring again. Otherwise, employees will not see an improvement in the control environment, leaving them wondering when the next fraud will occur.

**Engage in Fraud Auditing**

An excellent way to minimize fraud opportunities is to make it well known that the company operates a fraud auditing team. This group cycles through all departments of the organization, regularly looking for any hint of fraud. When employees routinely see this investigative team going about their work, they will realize that there is a reasonable chance of being caught if they ever engage in fraudulent activities. The fraud auditing team may never actually spot a case of fraud; the key point, however, is that employees are deterred from engaging in fraud because they believe they *might* be caught.

A good way for a fraud auditing team to increase its effectiveness is to constantly juggle the timing and type of examinations that it conducts. By doing so, employees will always be uncertain about the next time an internal auditor might appear in their department, and which areas they might audit. Otherwise, employees might attempt to engage in fraud during the intervals when they do not believe an audit team will be on-site.

## Fraud Detection – Symptoms

Fraudulent activities can be quite difficult to spot directly, since they may be concealed and the proportion of fraudulent transactions is likely to be quite low. An alternative way to identify fraud is indirectly – by being alert for the symptoms of fraud. These symptoms can come in many forms, such as:

- *Accounting anomalies.* A key supporting document for a large expenditure is missing or has been altered.
- *Analytical anomalies.* A routine analysis of trend lines and ratios detects an odd spike or decline in the data.
- *Lifestyle symptoms.* An employee arrives at work one day with a sports car that he should not be able to afford.
- *Unusual behavior.* An employee starts working much longer hours.

In the following sub-sections, we explain the nature of these fraud symptoms.

## Accounting Anomalies

The typical organization uses a certain set of accounting transactions that do not vary much over time, requiring roughly the same accounts and calling for the same types of supporting documents. When there are differences from these baseline transactions, there is a good chance that the anomalies are indicators of fraud. Here are a number of examples of accounting anomalies that could be symptoms of fraud:

- *Altered documents.* There may be an unusual number of instances in which accounting documents have been manually altered with crossed-out figures that have been replaced by different amounts. This could indicate that some-one in the accounting department is modifying documents to hide the theft of assets.
- *High-volume credits.* When there are many credits in the accounts receivable records, it can indicate that the accounting staff is intercepting payments from customers and then covering their tracks by creating credits to reduce the bal-ances in the customer accounts.
- *Increase in aged receivables.* When the collections department appears to be unable to collect on an increasing proportion of receivables, it is possible that some of those invoices are fakes. They may have been constructed internally to create sales that never actually occurred.
- *Increased expenses.* Someone could steal cash and then charge the amount to expense. This approach works well for fraud, since expense accounts are flushed out at year-end, so that the record of the theft does not persist in the account past year-end. When fraud occurs, charges are usually made to large-expense accounts, such as the cost of goods sold, so that a few thousand dol-lars of expense will not be detected through an analytical analysis.

---

**DISCUSSION**

When someone steal assets from a business and wants to hide the theft in the accounting rec-ords, the best place to do the hiding is indicated by the *accounting equation*, which is:

$$Assets = Liabilities + Equity$$

This equation is duplicated in the organization's balance sheet, where the total of all assets equals the sum of all liabilities and all equity.

So, if a person steals assets, how can the theft be hidden, so that the accounting equation in the balance sheet still balances? If assets decline due to theft, the choices are:

- *Reduce liabilities.* Reducing liabilities would continue to balance the balance sheet, but creditors would complain when the company does not pay its bills.
- *Reduce equity.* Reducing equity would continue to balance the balance sheet, but there are very few transactions within the equity area, so an adjusting entry in this area would be immediately obvious.

- *Reduce sales*. If sales are artificially reduced, this decreases profits, which in turn decreases equity, and thereby keeps the balance sheet in balance. However, a reduction in sales is usually investigated, since this area is subject to trend line analysis.
- *Increase expenses*. An increase in expenses decreases profits, which in turn decreases equity, and thereby keeps the balance sheet in balance. If the expense account chosen for this entry is a large one, the percentage change in the account will be small, and so may never be investigated.

In short, the best way for someone to hide an asset theft is by charging the amount of the expense to an expense account.

---

- *Last-minute entries*. Management may be targeting a specific profit figure to report at the end of a reporting period. If so, they may mandate that a journal entry be created that ensures that the target figure is achieved. This journal entry is likely to be one of the last journal entries in a period, since all other entries must first be made before it is possible to determine the shortfall for which fake profits must be manufactured.
- *Missing documents*. There may be no supporting documents that explain why a transaction occurred. For example, there would normally be a customer purchase order associated with an internal sales order. If not, it is possible that an employee made up the sales order, with the intent of having goods shipped to a dummy corporation.
- *Old reconciling items*. Most reconciling items on a bank statement will clear out within one or two months, such as uncleared checks or deposits in transit. When items linger on the reconciliation for a longer period of time, it could indicate a problem. For example, if a check paid to a supplier is not cashed for several months, it is possible that the supplier does not exist.
- *Rewritten records*. Employees may claim that they are rewriting records in order to eliminate errors or make the documents easier to read. What they may actually be doing is completely altering the documents in order to cover up a fraud.
- *Unsupported journal entries*. Someone could alter an account balance in order to bring the actual amount of assets on hand into agreement with the amount stated in the books. If so, they will have a difficult time creating any kind of supporting document that states the reason for the journal entry, and so may provide no supporting documentation at all.

The bulk of the issues underlying accounting anomalies have their origins within the accounting department, since few others have access to the accounting records. This means that someone within the department is engaged in fraud. Consequently, anyone investigating accounting anomalies will have to be exceedingly careful in their investigations, since the person engaged in fraud could be sitting next to them.

## Analytical Anomalies

An excellent way to detect fraud is to keep track of a variety of financial and operational metrics over a long period of time. The activity level of almost any measure should not vary all that much over time, so when there is a sudden change in a measure, this is certainly grounds for an investigation. Here are several examples of analytical anomalies:

- *Bad debt reductions.* A company that focuses hard on its profitability is reporting very low bad debts as a percentage of sales. The accounting department achieves this low figure by not keeping the reserve for bad debts at an adequate level, and also by delaying the recognition of bad debts. The result is a low bad debt expense, coupled with an inordinately high accounts receivable balance (since bad debts have not been flushed out of it).
- *Budgeting perfection.* A company consistently budgets aggressively for more sales and profits, and has an amazing ability to almost perfectly meet those numbers, period after period. Further investigation reveals that the management team is using whatever type of reporting fraud it takes to meet the budgeted targets in every reporting period.
- *Commodity price differs from market.* A business uses a large amount of plastic pellets as direct materials in its plastic molding operations. A routine comparison of commodity market prices to the prices paid to the company's pellet supplier finds that there was a modest divergence between the market price and actual price paid, starting one year ago. This could indicate a kickback situation between the supplier and the company's buyer assigned to the acquisition of plastic pellets.
- *Comparison of inventory value to volume.* The internal auditors of a wood products company evaluate the amount of finished boards that were supposedly in stock at year-end by calculating the approximate volume of boards that would be required to match the amount of ending inventory valuation that the auditee claims. This calculation reveals that the amount of inventory claimed would overwhelm the existing storage facilities. Clearly, management has been overstating the amount of ending inventory.
- *Fixed asset increases.* The internal auditors of a manufacturing firm routinely calculate the ratio of fixed assets to sales, to see if the proportion changes significantly from year to year. They discover that this proportion has spiked in the past year, indicating a surge in fixed assets. Further investigation reveals that the controller has been capitalizing expenditures that would normally have been charged to expense, resulting in an increase in profits just sufficient to earn the management team a hefty performance-based bonus.
- *Industry comparison.* A business continually reports increasing sales and profits, despite an industry-wide slump. In this situation, competitors are likely to be cutting prices in order to preserve their market share, which means that everyone in the industry is just trying to maintain sales levels while also reporting lower profits. For someone to both increase sales *and* profits in the face of such competitor actions is quite unlikely.

- *Inventory count corrections.* A company uses an incremental daily inventory count (cycle count), which is resulting in a large number of adjustments to the book balance of the inventory. The preponderance of these adjustments are downward, and almost entirely in the area of finished goods; that is, counts are verifying that the book balances of raw materials items are accurate most of the time. The situation indicates that someone might be stealing finished goods from the warehouse.
- *Low quality materials.* A company has been experiencing a number of product failures in the field, so it traces the issue back through the production process, eventually finding that a supplier is delivering low-quality raw materials. By tracing the customer complaints back in time, the internal audit manager believes that the low quality goods began to be shipped at about the time a new receiving manager was hired. This may indicate that the supplier has been paying kickbacks to the receiving manager to overlook low-quality deliveries.
- *Rapid rollouts in emerging markets.* Emerging markets have a well-earned reputation for being rife with corruption. This means that any organization wanting to do business in one of these countries will likely need to pay bribes in order to achieve a rapid rollout of their operations. Thus, when a rapid rollout *does* occur, it could be due less to the business acumen of the local manager and more to the size of the bribes paid. This red flag is especially true when a business miraculously obtains permits and licenses in short order.
- *Small amounts of overtime.* A review of overtime records finds that most employees incur overtime only at long intervals – except for one person, who routinely charges a half-hour of overtime, once or twice a week. This small amount falls below the overtime approval threshold for the business, so there is a possibility that the employee is reporting the overtime without actually working the extra hours.
- *Spike in expenses.* A trend line analysis of legal costs finds that legal expenditures jumped two years ago by 20%, and have stayed at that level since. There have been no unusual lawsuits or public company filings during that time, so it is possible that one or more law firms are overbilling the company.
- *Supplier billings too low.* A review of invoicing volumes by supplier finds that there are ten suppliers whose billings to the company never exceed $99. Since the invoice approval threshold for the business is $100, these smaller invoices are always paid automatically. Further investigation reveals that eight of the ten suppliers were added within the past year. The circumstances indicate that an employee might have set up a series of dummy corporations, and is using them to fraudulently bill the company at a level that will not be detected.

Analytical anomalies cannot always be detected if a fraud has been running for a long time. The reason is that an internal auditor might be looking for unusual changes in a trend line, but if the fraud has been running for the entire duration of the trend line, the data will appear to be quite normal.

Another issue with analytics is that managers know these analytics will be run by the internal audit department, and so may alter the financial information to conform to the expectations of the auditors. Consequently, it may take a detailed analysis of analytics in multiple areas to discern whether there may be a problem.

**Lifestyle Symptoms**

Employees who are engaged in fraud would require an immense amount of self-control to steal from their employer and not spend the money in some visible way. Instead, there is usually some evidence of a change in lifestyle. Here are several examples of lifestyle symptoms:

- Gambling trips to Las Vegas
- The replacement of an older car with a much nicer one
- Upgrades to an employee's house, or shifting to an entirely new one
- Taking up an expensive hobby, such as sailing or heli-skiing
- Stories of gifts made to friends and family

A common excuse given for a suddenly more profligate lifestyle is that a person has inherited wealth. If so, a reasonable question is why the person continues to work at the company. This is a particular concern when the individual refuses to take any vacation time or refuses to be promoted, which can indicate that they are covering up a fraud situation.

**Unusual Behavior**

When a person commits fraud, he will be under an increased level of stress. This can lead to changes in the person's behavior in the office, which may be extreme enough to be clearly visible to co-workers. Examples are:

- More variable mood swings
- A high level of suspicion of others
- Defensiveness
- Uses intimidation to keep others from investigating
- Uses excuses to an excessive degree
- A higher level of security, such as locked filing cabinets or office doors
- Working longer hours
- Extensive amounts of drinking, smoking, and drug use

Combinations of several of the preceding items can be particular indicators that a person is engaged in some kind of fraud.

## Fraud Detection – Assistance in Spotting Fraud

The internal auditor does not have to work alone when attempting to spot instances of fraud. Other people both within and outside of the organization can be encouraged to assist, as noted in the following sub-sections.

## Assistance from Employees

One way to detect fraud is to rely upon fellow employees to spot issues and bring them to the attention of management. Employees are in the best position to see someone engaged in fraud, or attempting to cover it up, or spending the proceeds, since they are on-site year-round. For example:

- An employee may return to work late at night and see someone engaged in a suspicious activity.
- Employees have access to all company records at various times, and so have an excellent opportunity to notice when supporting documentation is incorrect or missing.
- Employees will notice changes in the lifestyles of their fellow employees, such as vehicle or clothing upgrades.

In short, employees are ideal fraud witnesses.

To maximize the use of employees for fraud detection, it is necessary to educate the staff regarding indicators of fraud, so that they will be more inclined to notice suspicious activity. They must also be provided with a means of contacting management that does not result in any negative repercussions for themselves. In addition, the general environment for forwarding information should be made as easy as possible. Employees could fear reprisals for being whistle-blowers, so every effort should be made to mitigate these concerns, with a particular emphasis on keeping all tips private. As noted next, one of the best ways for employees to leave tips is the hotline.

## The Employee Hotline

An essential ingredient in a system that relies upon employee input is a fraud hotline. This is usually the best single method for detecting fraud. These hotlines do not require an employee to identify himself, which greatly reduces the risk of adverse consequences for the whistleblower. Ideally, the person receiving a hotline contact should be an independent third party, such as a company that specializes in providing hotline services. This supplier then reports issues to the company's board of directors or its audit committee. By using an outsider, there is no risk that the person receiving the call will be the individual committing fraud.

## Assistance from Auditors

Outside auditors are not good at spotting fraud, since they are on-site for only a short period of time, during which frauds usually stop. Also, auditors only conduct sample tests, which are not designed to detect fraud; instead, auditors are only looking for material misstatements in the financial statements. Consequently, they are far less likely to detect fraud than employees. Nonetheless, auditors may occasionally make note of puzzling transactions that turn out to be evidence of fraud, or are approached by employees with tips. Thus, though auditors are not the best source of information for fraud, they can provide occasional clues about the possible existence of fraud.

## Fraud Investigative Techniques

One way to investigate fraud is to delve into the motivations of a suspect, looking for any perceived pressures, fraud opportunities, or rationalizations that the person might have mentioned to a third party, or which anyone might have observed. For example, a person might have mentioned the pressure of coming up with enough money to pay for a child's college education, or he might have expressed dissatisfaction with having been passed over for a promotion.

An alternative approach is to focus on the fraud itself. One option is to try to catch the person in the act of committing fraud. This can be quite difficult, so an alternative is to examine those records that an individual might have altered in order to hide the evidence of their activities, and then reconstruct how the fraud was perpetrated. A third approach is to examine the lifestyle and personal records of the suspect to determine how any stolen funds or other assets might have been used.

The investigative method chosen should be tailored to the type of fraud that appears to have been committed. Some methods are especially effective when applied to certain types of fraud, as noted in the following example.

---

**EXAMPLE**

An anonymous tip reveals that there is a ghost employee in the company – specifically, in the maintenance department. Mr. Jones retired from the maintenance department a year ago, and yet he appears to still be drawing a paycheck. Since there is no physical loss of assets, consulting surveillance will not be helpful. Instead, the internal audit staff determines the account number into which paychecks for Mr. Jones are being deposited, and works with the local bank to determine the owner of the account – which turns out to be one of the payroll clerks.

**EXAMPLE**

Mule Corporation, maker of Bad Ass motorcycles, is suffering from losses in the tool area of its maintenance department. The tool storage area is locked and only three people have the key, so the list of suspects is gratifyingly short. The fraud investigation team elects to install a microscopic video camera in the cage to monitor tool check-outs and returns, and finds that the newest hire into the department has been making off with a few tools during the third shift.

**EXAMPLE**

A routine review of commodity prices finds that there has been a suspicious increase in the prices paid for certain commodities above their normal market prices. All of these commodities are under the control of Q.T. Smythe, one of the senior buyers. There is no direct evidence that a kickback scheme may be in progress, so the internal audit staff instead decides to compile evidence that Mr. Smythe's lifestyle has increased substantially since the presumed start of the kickback scheme. This includes a before-and-after examination of mortgages and other loans being paid off.

The team also works with the local law enforcement authorities to have wiretaps installed on his phone. They examine his prior e-mail records to see if there are any incriminating conversations with suppliers, interview both current and former buyers who have worked for the company, and interview suppliers unrelated to the current investigation to see if they have been solicited for kickbacks.

---

The type of investigatory techniques used should initially be restricted to those that will not trigger suspicion by the subject of the investigation, so that the team can collect information without fear of having any evidence destroyed. For example, e-mail records can be examined from the information technology department, while public records can be reviewed over the Internet or at a local government facility.

Once the team has accumulated more information and there appears to be a solid case, it can engage in more visible activities. This may first involve interviews with people who no longer work for the company or who work for other companies, since they are least likely to warn the suspect. Once information has been collected from the less-visible sources, the investigation escalates to include an interview with the person under suspicion. By the time the interview takes place, the team should have a solid case that does not allow the suspect any room to wriggle away from the accusation.

A key step in deciding upon the course of an investigation is to first develop an overview chart that summarizes what might have been stolen, who had an opportunity to steal the assets, and other speculations, such as:

- How the assets might have been stolen
- How the theft might have been concealed
- How the assets might have been converted into cash
- What types of fraud symptoms might be displayed by a suspect
- What kinds of pressure the suspects might be under to trigger the theft
- What types of rationalizations the suspects might have employed

Having all of this information in one place makes it easier to scan through the possible perpetrators, how they engaged in fraud, and why they did it. One can then more easily determine the best course of action for the fraud investigation. A sample fraud overview chart for a theft of consumer goods inventory is noted in the following exhibit.

## Fraud Overview Chart

| Item Stolen | Who had Opportunity | How Stolen? | How Concealed? | Conversion to Cash? | Fraud Symptoms? | Triggering Pressures? | Possible Rationalizing |
|---|---|---|---|---|---|---|---|
| Cell phones | Warehouse staff | Removed from boxes in warehouse | Re-tape boxes | Fenced on eBay | Incorrect inventory records | New car | Greed |
| | Shipping staff | Removed during palletization | Hole in center of pallet loads | Same | Customer complaints | Tax liens | Not promoted |
| | Delivery staff | Extracted while in transit | Claim theft from truck | Same | Customer complaints | Student loans | Feels underpaid |

As an example of the logic used in the preceding fraud overview chart, one possible suspect is the company's shipping staff. Several of them have tax liens outstanding against them (for which the garnishment information is available from the human resources department), and there was a recent promotion in the group that could have annoyed several people who were passed over for the promotion. To engage in the theft, they could have repositioned boxes of cell phones on the pallets, so there is a hole in the center that is not readily discernible. This represents a complete scenario for how and why a fraud might have been perpetrated.

## Documentary Evidence

Documentary evidence is collected from physical and electronic records. This usually involves the manual examination of documents, but can also include automated searches of electronic records to look for anomalies or other indicators of fraud. Documents can also be subjected to a variety of analyses, such as examining financial statements to see if there are indicators that the underlying accounting records have been altered.

## Personal Observation

Investigators may engage in the direct surveillance of suspects or other similar activities to collect information. These activities usually involve either viewing or listening to suspects or the activities that appear to be related to a suspected fraud. The key types of surveillance are:

- *Electronic observation.* This most commonly involves the use of video recording equipment, which is a common emplacement in areas where there is a high risk of theft. Wiretapping is only allowed for duly authorized law enforcement personnel.
- *Following the persons in question.* This involves tailing the individuals in question, with the intent of identifying additional individuals who may be involved in a fraud.
- *From a fixed location.* This involves having one or more people set up at a location from which they can observe the activity in question. They then take notes or record the activity. Notes should include a complete time log of what was observed.

When someone is engaged in personal observation, the intent is to catch a perpetrator in the act. There is no intent to investigate how a fraud is being concealed or how the proceeds are spent because there is no need to do so – witnessing a fraud is far better evidence than compiling circumstantial evidence about it.

Personal observation is an expensive technique, so its use may be limited by the investigatory budget. Given its cost, this approach is usually limited to situations in which the amount of loss is suspected to be high, or when other alternative approaches have failed.

### Physical Evidence

The collection of physical evidence includes an examination for fingerprints, identification numbers on stolen property, tire tracks, and any other types of tangible evidence related to fraudulent activities. The collection of physical evidence is relatively rare in fraud cases, with the exception of the theft of fixed assets or inventory. In other cases where cash is stolen or financial results are manipulated, there is little physical evidence to obtain.

## The Role of Internal Auditing

Clearly, the internal audit department has a substantial role in advising management about the prevention and detection of fraud, as well as in the investigation of any alleged cases of fraud. This can require a specialized level of expertise that the average internal auditor may not possess, so some of the prevention and detection work could be outsourced to a specialist. Nonetheless, one should exercise a reasonable degree of professional care by considering where fraud could arise within an organization, as well as by advising on prevention techniques that could mitigate the risk of fraud. Further, the department could develop data analysis tools that are used to routinely scan company data for signs of fraud schemes; this can detect fraud in its early stages, before the company loses substantial sums. Internal audit staffers may also conduct presentations around the company in fraud awareness training, so that employees can spot instances of fraud and warn management. In addition, the internal audit manager should periodically discuss with the board the potential for the occurrence of fraud within the organization, as well as how fraud risk is currently being managed. This discussion may include a presentation about emerging fraud issues that could impact the company.

In essence, the essential role of the internal auditor relating to fraud is to act as an advisor to the board, pointing out fraud risks, how they are being monitored, where there are shortfalls, and what to do about them. If the board wants the department to engage more fully in the prevention and detection of fraud, it will likely need to authorize the expenditure of additional funds to ensure that internal auditors are fully equipped with the necessary skills to do so.

**Note:** If there is one facet of the internal auditor's job that requires the healthy use of skepticism, it is in the investigation of fraud, since this is where employees are most likely to cover their tracks and divert attention to the greatest extent possible in order to avoid detection of any fraud schemes they are running.

## Summary

Fraud can result in massive losses for an organization and its investors, so it is imperative for the internal audit department to play a large role in advising the board about fraud risks and how they are being mitigated within the organization. This requires a significant knowledge of fraud indicators and fraud prevention and detection techniques. Internal auditors may also be called upon to conduct investigations when fraud is suspected, though specialists are sometimes called in to assist with or run these inquiries.

# Chapter 8
# Internal Audit Management

## Introduction

The internal auditing function plays a critical assurance and consulting role within an organization, so it must be properly managed in order to maximize its effectiveness. In this chapter, we focus on those unique aspects of management that pertain solely to an internal audit department. The text covers such issues as the unique positioning of the department within an organization, the responsibilities of the internal audit manager, quality assurance, and internal audit metrics.

## Organizational Positioning

For the internal auditing function to independently evaluate the rest of the organization, it needs to occupy an unusual position within the business. It should report directly to the board of directors or its audit committee, thereby reducing the influence of the senior management team on the department. If this is not done, and the department instead reports to a senior manager, then it will not have the objectivity to provide independent evaluations of company operations.

The department can be properly protected with a charter that defines its purpose, authority, and responsibilities. As long as the charter clearly states the reporting relationship of the department, senior management cannot interfere with it. An annual internal audit plan is then used to expand upon the charter, stating the tasks that the department plans to engage in during the upcoming year. Based on these foundational documents, the internal audit manager then develops a set of policies and procedures to delineate how the department is to conduct its day-to-day activities.

## Departmental Evaluation

The board or its audit committee should conduct an assessment of the internal audit department on an annual basis. This assessment is based on the department's charter and annual plan, where actual results are compared to its mission and any shortfalls are discussed. This evaluation can also include a discussion of whether the department has sufficient resources to fulfill its responsibilities in an adequate manner, which may result in an altered budget for the following year. In short, the board needs to ensure that the department is as effective as possible.

## Responsibilities of the Internal Audit Manager

The internal audit manager has a number of responsibilities that vary significantly from what is expected of a manager in any other department. These unique responsibilities are as follows:

- *Charter oversight.* The manager should periodically assess whether the department's charter is sufficient for its role within the company, which may require periodic changes to the charter. By comparison, most departments do not have a charter at all.
- *Independence and objectivity.* The manager needs to monitor whether the internal audit staff is truly able to conduct itself with a proper level of objectivity and independence from the rest of the organization. Any number of situations could degrade this ability, and may require corrective action. For example:
  - o Internal auditors should not conduct assessments of operations for which they were previously responsible until at least a year has passed.
  - o Internal auditors should not conduct assessments when they have a conflict of interest.
  - o Internal auditors should not accept gifts from the parties they are assessing.
  - o Internal auditors should not perform operating activities or design processes that they may be called upon to assess.

- *Interference.* The manager needs to watch out for any cases in which company employees are interfering with the department's work, either in restricting the scope of its investigations, performing work, or communicating its findings, and inform the board or its audit committee about these issues.
- *Proficiency.* The internal audit staff may require quite a substantial amount of training and experience in order to conduct its assigned assessment and consulting engagements properly. The manager needs to decide when extra training is needed, as well as when to bring in outside experts to assist with the department's various projects.
- *Planning.* Though all departments compile periodic plans of activities, they are usually copied from the prior year's plans with only slight adjustments. This is not the case for the internal audit manager, who will likely compile a substantially different plan for the department every year. Each plan is based on the most recent assessment of key risks within the organization, which are then ranked and associated with assurance and consulting engagements to assess how well the business is managing the risks. Furthermore, the plan may change over the course of the year, as the risk profile of the organization changes and the manager receives requests for consulting services from around the company. A likely outcome is a baseline annual plan, for which quarterly updates are issued.

The department plan should be quite extensive in terms of staff planning, and to a much greater extent than is found in other departments. There should be an engagement schedule, stating when each project is supposed to begin and end, as well as specific assignments to each engagement, based on the expertise of the staff. These assignments should be quite specific for at least the next quarter, when staff availability is most predictable.

The annual plan and any revisions to it should be presented to the board or audit committee for approval. When presented, the plan should include a list of all proposed engagements, why they were picked, and the objectives and scope of each engagement. This information is needed so that directors can properly evaluate the plan and see if it accords with their perceptions of the risks that need to be assessed.

The consulting engagements accepted by the department should be considered secondary to the assurance engagements that are the primary task of the department. If assurance engagements are not completed, the company is laying itself open to risks that could result in severe losses. Conversely, not engaging in a consulting engagement is more likely to result in the loss of lesser efficiencies that will not have anywhere near as large a financial impact on the business. However, when the resources are available to do so, the department should take on consulting engagements based on how well these projects could mitigate risks, enhance profits, or improve its operations.

## Just-in-Time Audit Scheduling

The use of an annual audit plan leaves no scheduling space for rush audit requests. A rush request typically arises when there is a control breach or a need for advice regarding a systems change. These requests usually must be addressed in short order, which requires substantial last-minute changes to the department work schedule.

A mid-way measure that accommodates the need for rush projects is to block out a significant part of the full annual schedule well in advance, while deliberately leaving a number of time periods open. This approach allows one to accommodate a number of priority projects without an undue number of changes to the overall work schedule. The result is a company that has a good impression of the responsiveness of the internal audit department, as well as a work schedule that, by and large, does not require much shifting of priorities.

# Departmental Structure

There are several ways to design the structure of the internal audit department. One approach is to adopt a flat structure, where there is a minimal hierarchy within the department. Instead, most people have the same title and approximately the same experience and skill level. This approach requires a reduced amount of supervisory time, since most employees have a high skill level. A flat structure also tends to result in reduced employee turnover, since there is no need for office politics to pursue promotional opportunities. However, the relatively high skill level needed in a flat structure typically results in higher average compensation levels, which can be expensive for the company.

An alternative approach is to adopt a hierarchical structure, where junior internal auditors with relatively minimal skill sets are assigned to more senior auditors, from whom they can gain experience. In this structure, there may be several internal auditor job positions, such as the following:

- *Staff auditor.* Performs fieldwork on a variety of assurance and consulting engagements.
- *Senior auditor.* Plans engagements, oversees the activities of staff auditors, performs fieldwork, reviews workpapers, and evaluates staff auditor performance.
- *Audit manager.* Supervises audit and consulting engagements, as well as conducting risk assessments, maintaining the annual audit plan, and overseeing the work of senior auditors. This is the department manager in smaller organizations.
- *Audit director.* Develops and administers the audit plan, interacts with the audit committee, and supervises audit managers. Only present in larger internal audit departments.
- *Chief audit executive.* Administers the entire internal audit department, supervising audit managers and audit directors. Only present in larger internal audit departments.

There may also be a number of auditor specialist positions, such as IT auditors, actuaries and data analysts, depending on the needs of the department and the work it is asked to perform.

Under the hierarchical approach, the intent is to continually train and then promote people into more senior positions, though this concept only works when more senior personnel are routinely moving out of their positions (presumably back into the organization in other roles).

## Staffing Issues

The staffing of engagements can be unusually difficult in the internal auditing arena. The problem is that each engagement requires a particular skill set, and no auditor can be expected to have every skill needed to fulfill the requirements of every possible engagement. The result is a great deal of advance planning to ensure that every engagement is properly staffed with a knowledgeable group of auditors. This may require the scheduling of extensive training prior to some engagements, or the hiring of specialist contractors, or bringing in more senior people to instruct staff auditors in more specialized knowledge areas.

One way to improve the efficiency of the staff is to provide them with administrative support, so that they can spend more time on the field work that generates the most value for the organization. For example, tasks related to recruiting, managing the department schedule, performing data analytics analysis, and performing internal quality assurance reviews could be handed off to specialists. This is only an option in larger internal audit departments, where the volume of work makes specialization cost-effective.

As just noted, proper staffing requires training. This can be accomplished either by actively recruiting for the required skill sets, or by conducting an extensive training program for the staff. The department can also track the continuing professional education requirements of those personnel who have professional certifications (such as the Certified Internal Auditor certification) to ensure that they maintain their professional training requirements. Training can be combined with the department's succession planning, so that promotions will not occur until an auditor has completed a required set of training programs.

The audit committee should be kept informed of the training situation in the department, since this directly impacts the ability of the internal auditors to conduct engagements in a proficient manner. Whenever there is a shortfall, the audit committee should be asked to assign extra resources to the department, either to provide additional training or to hire in the necessary personnel.

---

**Tip:** The department should have an auditor skills matrix. This matrix can be as simple as a set of auditor resumes that are updated after each engagement has been completed. A more usable system is to load auditor skills and experience into a database that can be searched with key words. Doing so makes it easier to populate an engagement with personnel who have the most relevant skills and experience, without having to manually search through a large number of resumes.

---

## Quality Assurance

The department needs to have a system for monitoring its adherence to internal auditing standards, as well as the efficiency and effectiveness of its activities. Quality assurance can be conducted by a qualified, independent party, or it may be initially conducted internally and then verified by a qualified, independent party. This independent peer review should be completed at least once every five years.

A quality assurance program investigates how well the department conforms with the IIA's standards and its code of ethics, as well as how well the department corrects for any issues of nonconformance that are found. It also evaluates the adequacy of the department's charter, objectives, policies, and procedures, noting any issues requiring remediation. The program also examines how well the department supports the company's governance, risk management, and system of controls, noting any areas of improvement. Further, it investigates the department's compliance with all applicable laws and regulations, noting instances in which there have been repeated compliance failures. Finally, it notes how readily the department adopts best practices to continually enhance its operations. The end result of this program is a listing of deficiencies and recommendations for improvement; the recommendations will be checked during the next peer review to see how well they have been implemented. A report on the review is issued to the board and senior management, noting the scope and frequency of these assessments, the conclusions reached, and any corrective action plans.

An internally-based quality assessment can involve a number of activities, such as mandating peer reviews of engagement workpapers by auditors directly involved in an engagement, gaining feedback from internal customers, and benchmarking the department's processes against acknowledged internal auditing best practices.

---

**Tip:** Performing an internal assessment just before an independent peer review is conducted can reduce the time and cost of the peer review, since any issues found can be remediated before the peer review begins.

---

## The Internal Audit Library

When an internal audit team conducts an audit of any aspect of a company's operations, they tend to treat the conditions they find in isolation. They may not be aware of similar conditions elsewhere in the company, and may encounter a technical issue with which they are not familiar. These issues can be mitigated by creating an online internal audit library that is stocked with information from all prior internal audit engagements. The library can also contain references to who worked on these earlier audits, and their contact information. Further, the library can include the most updated accounting and auditing standards, for reference purposes. With some additional work, the library can even contain a listing of the most common issues found on audits, and what corrective actions were taken to mitigate or eliminate the issues. A well-maintained on-line internal audit library can contribute to the efficiency of new audits by reducing the amount of research time used by internal auditors. A considerable amount of labor is required to create such a library. Consider the following tasks:

- An electronic form must be filled out once each audit is completed, containing all of the information required to populate the library.
- The same form must be completed for all earlier audits that were completed before the library project was initiated.
- Obtain an on-line subscription to the latest accounting and auditing standards, which should include a comprehensive search capability.

This approach will only work if the audit staff understands the need for the library, and is willing to spend the time required to create and update it.

## Budget Issues

Theoretically, the staffing of the internal audit department should be increased to the point where the marginal benefit obtained from its last assurance or consulting engagement equals the marginal cost of that engagement. In reality, the department tends to be smaller than that optimal level. It tends to begin as quite a small department, and is incrementally increased to meet the most pressing needs of the organization. Staffing additions tend to be in response to risk events that cause large losses, which means that budget increases tend to be in reaction to negative events, rather than as a result of an analysis of marginal utility to the organization. Consequently, there are always more prospective engagements for the department than it can reasonably handle. Because of this lack of supply and excess of demand, planning has to concentrate on only performing the most critical engagements; below a certain threshold level, the department simply does not have the resources to complete any additional work.

It is possible to make more effective use of the funds allocated to the department by coordinating its activities with those of other assurance and consulting service providers that are working with the company. The intent is to avoid any duplication of work, so that the department is focused on areas that have not been addressed by other parties. This involves ongoing discussions and information sharing with such parties as government regulators, the firm's external auditors, and other assurance teams within the company – such as those involved in quality assurance. When duplicative activities are eliminated from the audit plan, this allows the department to engage in additional assurance and consulting service engagements that would otherwise have been impossible, given the resources available.

> **Note:** The coordination of activities includes sending the department's audit plans and engagement results to these other parties, so that they can adjust their assurance and consulting engagement plans accordingly.

When the department is coordinating its activities with those of other assurance and consulting service providers, the board should be kept apprised of the situation, so that it understands who is assessing which risks, and the outcomes of those engagements.

## Internal Audit Metrics

A consistently-applied set of metrics should be formulated and periodically calculated for the department. The intent is to make note of any performance issues that may arise over time, and which should be investigated further. Possible metrics to consider include the following:

- *Customer satisfaction.* This is obviously a qualitative measurement, and could be more reflective of a pleasant relationship with a customer than an effective one. Still, it can be useful for judging relations with the various business units.
- *Internal auditor turnover rate.* This is useful for judging how well new applicants are screened for the job, as well as how the department trains, mentors, and treats new recruits.
- *Lead time to fulfill audit requests.* This is an indicator of whether the department has an appropriate match between its resources and the demands placed upon them.
- *Percentage of auditors with certification.* This can be useful for judging the level of auditor expertise within the department.
- *Plan accomplishment.* This shows how well the department was able to follow through on the initial plan of activities, though it could mask the presence of audits that were cut short in order to achieve the measurement goal.

- *Recommendations accepted.* This shows the volume of recommendations accepted by management, though it does not reveal the quality of those recommendations.

## Board Reporting

Since the internal audit department is supposed to report to the board of directors or its audit committee, an essential component of managing the department is reporting to the board. The internal audit manager should report to the board on a regular basis, noting the department's performance relative to the annual plan, the risk issues found, control failures, governance issues, and essentially anything requiring the board's attention. This reporting should include any significant deviations from the audit plan, such as the completion (or not) of engagements, staffing shortfalls, budget overruns, and the reasons for them. In essence, the internal audit manager should provide status reports in the same manner that any other manager of another department would do to the senior manager to whom he or she reports.

The main difference between the reports of the internal audit department and those of other departments are that these reports should include significant engagement observations and recommendations. In those cases in which senior management has chosen not to implement a recommendation, the board should be informed, including a commentary on what this means to the risk profile of the organization.

## Summary

In this chapter, we covered the unique aspects of running the internal audit department. The internal audit manager needs to ensure that the department's charter is sufficiently robust to ensure the independence of the auditors, while also paying an unusual amount of attention to the level of expertise required for each scheduled engagement. The work of the department centers around its audit plan, which is used to schedule staffing assignments and training activities, so the manager needs to review the plan's status on a frequent basis – probably daily. Finally, this department is subject to a periodic quality assurance review, which ensures that the department is operating properly. It should be no surprise that these unique issues mirror those of a public accounting firm, which engages in many of the same activities.

# Chapter 9
## Audit Evidence

## Introduction

The internal auditor needs to gather sufficient appropriate audit evidence to develop high-quality assurance conclusions and consulting advice. This involves the collection of a broad range of audit evidence, which is one of the core activities of the auditor. In this chapter, we cover the nature of audit evidence, how it is collected, the concepts of relevance and reliability, and several related matters.

## The Nature of Audit Evidence

*Audit evidence* is any information used by the internal auditor as the basis for his or her conclusions. Audit evidence may be contained within the accounting records of an auditee, or it may be obtained elsewhere. Accounting records are the initial accounting entries and supporting records of an auditee, such as invoices, checks, contracts, journal entries, and ledgers, as well as spreadsheets, computations, and reconciliations. Audit evidence is obtained through a variety of activities, including inquiries, confirmations, inspections, observations, recalculations, and analytical procedures.

Alternative sources of audit evidence (that is, *not* from an auditee's accounting records) include previous engagements and the work of management's or auditor's specialists.

Audit evidence may also be obtained from the absence of information. For example, the refusal of the auditee to provide certain kinds of information constitutes a form of audit evidence.

Two aspects of audit evidence are its sufficiency and its appropriateness. The *sufficiency* concept relates to the quantity of audit evidence collected. Sufficiency is critical when there is a higher risk of control failures. The *appropriateness* concept relates to the quality of the evidence collected. The two aspects are interrelated, since a high level of appropriateness may allow the internal auditor to collect a smaller quantity of evidence (and vice versa). However, this concept does not always work, since obtaining more audit evidence does not necessarily compensate for a poor level of appropriateness.

The amount of audit evidence needed to support the auditor's opinion is cumulative in nature, so the amount of additional evidence compiled as an auditor proceeds is, in some part, derived from the results already obtained.

When using information that has been produced by the auditee, the auditor should determine whether the information is sufficiently reliable to serve as audit evidence. This means that the information should be sufficiently precise and detailed. In cases where the audit evidence obtained from one source is inconsistent with evidence obtained from another party, or when there is any doubt about its reliability, the auditor should determine what procedural changes will be needed to resolve the issue. A concern here is that the auditee may not have a clear understanding of the purpose or scope of the engagement, which may result in incorrect or out-of-scope information being provided to the auditor.

## Relevance and Reliability

The quality of the audit evidence obtained is impacted by the relevance and reliability of the underlying information. *Relevance* is the degree to which audit evidence is connected to the purpose of an audit procedure. For example, when testing to see if all shipments to customers have been billed, a comparison of the shipping log to the invoice register would be considered highly relevant. Conversely, testing to see if invoiced amounts match the auditee's official price list would not be relevant, since it does nothing to reveal any instances of missing invoices.

The *reliability* of audit evidence is influenced by its source, as well as the circumstances under which it was obtained. For example, a confirmation of a receivable balance obtained from someone other than the party to which the confirmation request was addressed calls into question its reliability. Or, a pension liability analysis prepared by a specialist who owns stock in the auditee reduces the reliability of the analysis. The following observations generally apply to the reliability of audit evidence:

- Reliability is increased when evidence is obtained from an independent third party.
- Reliability is increased when evidence obtained internally when the controls over its preparation and maintenance are strong.
- Reliability is increased when it is obtained through direct observation, rather than by inference.
- Reliability is increased when it is obtained in documentary form, rather than orally.
- Reliability is increased when it is provided by original documents, rather than copies or electronic versions.

## Reasonable Assurance

It would take the collection of a vast amount of audit evidence for an internal auditor to give the board absolute assurance that company's processes and controls are operating properly. Within the time constraints of the typical audit, even an experienced auditor can only collect sufficient evidence to provide reasonable assurance that systems are operating as intended. The amount of time and cost required to develop absolute assurance about one's conclusions would not be cost-effective, so the auditor is instead expected to give opinions that express reasonable assurance about the conclusions reached. This means that the auditor needs to be selective about finding audit evidence that is both reliable and pertinent to the objectives of the engagement.

## Professional Skepticism

When reviewing audit evidence, the internal auditor should always exercise a sufficient degree of professional skepticism. A properly skeptical auditor will be alert to the presence of contradictory audit evidence, any issues that question the reliability of auditee documents, conditions indicating the presence of fraud, and any circumstances calling for additional audit procedures. Maintaining a skeptical viewpoint is needed to mitigate the risks of overlooking unusual circumstances, over-generalizing when drawing conclusions, and using inappropriate assumptions.

---

**EXAMPLE**

An internal auditor is presented with a situation in which the sole supporting evidence for a bill and hold transaction is a written statement from a customer that it is authorizing the auditee to hold completed inventory on-site for the next year. There is no explanation for why the inventory is being held, and there is no provision for charging storage fees to the customer. The customer has unaccountably gone on vacation to Antarctica for the next month, and so cannot be reached. A reasonable degree of professional skepticism would suggest that this transaction is not really a sale.

---

An ongoing sense of skepticism allows an internal auditor to maintain an open viewpoint to form judgments based on the majority of audit evidence gathered.

## Audit Procedures

Audit evidence may be derived from many types of audit procedures, as noted in the following sub-sections. Audit procedures are employed during an engagement for the following reasons:

- To obtain sufficient appropriate audit evidence to achieve the stated audit objectives.
- To obtain a detailed understanding of the auditee.
- To test how well a business unit's system of internal controls has been designed and is functioning.
- To test both operational and financial data for errors and evidence of fraud.

When reviewing the following types of audit procedures, please note that one procedure may result in the achievement of more than one audit objective, while in other cases multiple audit procedures will be required to achieve a single audit objective. Also, some procedures are more expensive or time-consuming than others, so the auditor needs to be selective about which ones to employ.

Audit procedures must be applied within the correct period of time. Thus, an auditor seeking to test the effectiveness of a control over a specific period of time should make sure that any testing procedures conducted are for transactions occurring within the designated time period.

## Inspection

Another audit procedure is inspection, which involves the examination of an auditee's records or the physical inspection of its assets. For example, the internal auditor could inspect purchase orders for evidence of authorization, or inspect checks for evidence that they were appropriately signed. Or, the inspection of a sales contract could lead the auditor to conclusions about how the auditee should be recognizing the revenue associated with the contract. Perhaps the most common of all inspection activities is the auditor's participation in an auditee's physical inventory count process, where the auditor may review individual inventory items to verify their existence.

## Observation

Yet another audit procedure is the use of observation, which involves looking at a process that is being performed by auditee personnel. For example, the auditor could observe how an auditee's warehouse team conducts the year-end inventory count. However, there are several weaknesses in the observation concept; one is that being observed may alter the behavior of the persons carrying out a process, while another concern is that observations only deal with a specific point in time – the process being reviewed could change substantially at other times of the year.

## Confirmation

A high-quality source of audit evidence is the external confirmation. These are direct written responses to the internal auditor by an outside party, confirming such matters as receivable, payable, bank account, and loan balances. Confirmations are a highly-reliable form of audit evidence, since they are obtained from independent sources, and are more reliable than evidence that is obtained indirectly or by inference. The use of confirmations can be especially useful in obtaining audit evidence with a high degree of reliability, which may be needed when the auditor is investigating significant risks of control failures.

Though confirmations usually only deal with ending balances, the auditor can expand these requests to include the terms of agreements, or of any changes to those agreements.

## Vouching

The auditor can use *vouching*, which involves reviewing documentary evidence to see if it properly supports the item under examination, such as tracing a sample of inventory items in the accounting records to actual units in the warehouse, to see if they exist. Or, an auditor might examine a shipping document to see if it supports the amount of a sale recorded in the sales journal. When engaged in vouching, the auditor is looking for any errors in the amount recorded in the accounting or operations records, as well as ensuring that the transactions are recorded in the correct accounts. The auditor is also verifying that transactions have been properly authorized.

**Recalculation**

The auditor may choose to check the mathematical accuracy of an auditee's records, such as reperforming a bank reconciliation to test whether it was completed correctly.

**Reperformance**

The auditor can elect to independently execute the procedures or controls associated with a targeted activity that had already been performed as part of the auditee's system of internal controls.

**Inquiry**

A mainstay activity is for the auditor to gather audit evidence through ongoing inquiries. The most effective inquiries result from discussions with knowledgeable persons, both within and outside of the auditee business unit, on the full range of audit topics being examined. Inquiries can cover a broad range of topics, such as asking whether there have been any cases in which management has overridden business unit controls, or whether there are any additional lease arrangements that do not appear in the financial statements. These results may lead the auditor to construct additional audit procedures to investigate topics that had not initially been main targets of the engagement.

Inquiries can also be useful for background information, such as understanding management's reasons for taking certain actions, or why it chose to stop pursuing certain activities.

**Analytical Procedures**

The auditor can engage in a series of evaluations of an auditee's financial information by comparing the relationships between various financial and operational information, such as sales per person or a historical trend analysis of the gross margin percentage. The intent is to identify fluctuations in these outcomes that are inconsistent with other relevant information, or that differ from expectations. This approach can also involve the use of benchmarking data, to see if an auditee's financial results and financial position are reasonable when compared to similar information for competitors. Examples of analytical procedures are as follows:

- *Sales.* Compare the total square footage of floor space to retail sales in prior periods and carry the relationship forward into the current period, multiplying the total average square footage of retail space in the current year to the historical amount of sales per square foot. Issues that may cause the outcome to vary from expectations include the presence of low-performing stores, changes in the mix of products being sold, and competitive pressures.
- *Receivables.* Compare the days outstanding metric to the amount for prior years. This relationship between receivables and sales should remain about the same over time, unless there have been changes in the customer base, the credit policy of the business unit, or its collection practices.

- *Inventory.* Compare inventory to the cost of sales within the current period to determine the efficiency with which inventory is used. This can also be plotted on a trend line to compare turnover over multiple reporting periods.
- *Asset usage.* Compare earnings before taxes to the average assets of the auditee over the reporting period, to derive the return on assets. This is used to determine how effectively assets are being used to generate earnings.
- *Payables.* Compare the ending payables balance to sales, to gain an understanding of the liquidity of the auditee.
- *Liquidity.* Review the current ratio over several reporting periods. This comparison of current assets to current liabilities should be about the same over time, unless the auditee has altered its policies related to accounts receivable, inventory, or accounts payable. A variation is to use the quick ratio instead, which excludes inventory from the numerator.
- *Bad debts.* Examine a trend line of bad debt expenses. This amount should vary in relation to sales. If not, management may not be correctly recognizing bad debts in a timely manner. A variation is to compare the bad debt expense to sales for the reporting period.
- *Compensation.* Multiply the number of employees by the average pay rate to estimate the total annual compensation, and then compare the result to the actual total compensation expense for the period. The auditee must explain any material difference from this amount, such as bonus payments or employee leave without pay.
- *Profitability.* Compare the gross margin to sales, and also compare net profits to sales. Doing so reveals the proportion of profits generated from a given volume of sales. These ratios can also be plotted on a trend line to show variations over time.

## Scanning

A variation on analytical procedures is for the auditor to scan auditee data to identify significant or unusual items to examine further, such as by examining unusual journal entries, general ledger balances, adjusting entries, suspense accounts, reconciliations, and so forth. The use of electronic scanning can be used to examine entire populations of auditee data for these anomalies. The results of these examinations constitute additional audit evidence. This approach also results in additional evidence, in that the auditor has exercised professional judgment in determining that the items not selected for further analysis are less likely to be misstated.

## Analytical Procedure Case Study

This section provides a case study for the Bigelow Burgers regional fast food chain, and illustrates the uses of analytical procedures. The primary emphasis of these analyses is on the sales figures being reported by Bigelow for each of its 10 stores. These 10 stores include one (Store 10) that was opened during the current reporting year. The operations of these stores are quite similar, though one store located near the company's headquarters is used as a test store that rolls out new product offerings before the other stores in the chain, and so has a larger menu. There is also some variability in the foot traffic experienced by each store, which directly impacts their sales. The relevant information for these stores appears in the following exhibit.

**Bigelow Burgers Information by Store**

| Store | Prior-Year Sales | Current-Year Sales | Dollar Change | Sales % Change | Current-Year Cost of Goods | CGS % | Square Feet | Sales / Sq. Ft. |
|---|---|---|---|---|---|---|---|---|
| 1 | $1,969,223 | $1,955,438 | -$13,785 | -0.7% | $1,218,238 | 62.3% | 6,200 | $315 |
| 2 | 1,640,825 | 1,734,352 | 93,527 | 5.7% | 863,707 | 49.8% | 5,200 | 334 |
| 3 | 1,529,602 | 1,629,026 | 99,424 | 6.5% | 816,142 | 50.1% | 4,800 | 339 |
| 4 | 1,562,858 | 1,592,552 | 29,694 | 1.9% | 775,573 | 48.7% | 4,200 | 379 |
| 5 | 1,402,092 | 1,460,980 | 58,888 | 4.2% | 715,880 | 49.0% | 4,400 | 332 |
| 6 | 1,317,099 | 1,280,220 | -36,879 | -2.8% | 651,632 | 50.9% | 4,000 | 320 |
| 7 | 1,680,842 | 1,719,501 | 38,659 | 2.3% | 882,104 | 51.3% | 5,400 | 318 |
| 8 | 1,213,049 | 1,253,080 | 40,031 | 3.3% | 626,540 | 50.0% | 3,800 | 330 |
| 9 | 1,713,581 | 1,895,221 | 181,640 | 10.6% | 1,002,572 | 51.4% | 5,400 | 351 |
| 10 | -- | 752,186 | 752,186 | --% | 397,906 | 52.9% | 4,200 | 179 |
| Total | $14,029,171 | $15,272,556 | $1,243,385 | 8.9% | $7,950,294 | 52.1% | 47,600 | $321 |
| w/o #10 | $14,029,171 | $14,520,370 | $491,199 | 3.5% | $7,552,388 | 52.0% | 43,400 | $335 |

Store 1 is the original company store, and is the one in which new products are always rolled out first. Store 10 was opened half-way through the current reporting year.

In this case study, the audit objective is to determine whether sales have been overstated, and the primary means for determining whether this is the case is the relationship between current-year and prior-year sales. The materiality threshold is considered to be a 6% change from the prior year. The expectation for current-year sales is the prior-year sales. The prior-year sales have been audited, while the current-year sales have *not* been audited.

**Trend Analysis**

To conduct a trend analysis, we strip out Store 10, since there is no prior-year history for it. Doing so results in the 3.5% year-to-year change that appears in the prior exhibit. At an aggregate level, this seems to indicate a reasonable increase. However, by disaggregating sales at the store level, we can see that Stores 3 and 9 have experienced sales increases that exceed the materiality threshold. The internal auditor should design procedures to investigate the sales for these two stores further. Possible considerations to investigate are whether the full product line has been rolled out within these stores, as well as variations in foot traffic between the stores.

**Ratio Analysis**

To conduct a ratio analysis, we compare the audited cost of goods sold percentage for the prior year to the current-year percentage. An unusually low cost of goods sold percentage could indicate that the reported sales for a store are too high. Though not stated in the preceding exhibit, the prior-year cost of goods sold percentage was 49.8% for all stores other than Store 1, which is the store used by corporate headquarters for new product rollouts. The acceptable difference for a store is considered to be 1.5%. Other than Store 1, this expectation is only exceeded by Stores 9 and 10. The auditor should design procedures to investigate the cost of sales for these two stores further. One possibility is that the newest stores have the least well-trained staff, and so dispose of more food than the personnel in the older stores.

**Reasonableness Test**

To conduct a reasonableness test, we compare the sales per square foot for each of the 10 stores to the industry average. The average sales per square foot for similar burger chains is $330/square foot. In the preceding year, all stores recorded sales per square foot that were within eight percent of this figure, so the expectation for the current year is for this analysis to yield results within 8% of the industry average.

The sales per square foot results are displayed in the preceding exhibit. In aggregate, the $335 of sales per square foot for all stores except Store 10 appear to indicate that the auditee's store sales are adhering closely to the industry average. However, when viewed at a disaggregated level, Store 4 has sales significantly higher than expected, in proportion to its square footage, which could warrant further review. Also, Store 10 was opened at mid-year, so its sales per square foot can be annualized by multiplying them by two, which results in sales per square foot of $358; this amount is higher than every other store except Store 4, and is especially suspicious when considering that it is also the newest store, and so should require a number of months to build up its sales volume. In short, both Stores 4 and 10 may require further investigation.

## Summary

When collecting audit evidence, the internal auditor is particularly concerned with the quality of the evidence collected, rather than its quantity. Thus, the auditor needs to continually examine evidence to see if it is relevant and reliable, and whether it is precisely targeted at the goals that the auditor wishes to achieve. Otherwise, it is possible that the auditor will conduct a large amount of work without really determining whether the objectives of an engagement have been attained.

# Chapter 10
# Internal Audit Working Papers

## Introduction

The internal auditor should prepare audit documentation, which is intended to provide evidence of his or her basis for a conclusion about whether engagement objectives have been met, and to show that the engagement was planned and performed in accordance with IIA standards, as well as any applicable legal and regulatory requirements. In addition to this evidentiary focus, internal audit documentation can also be useful in the following areas:

- Supporting the engagement team in planning and implementing the engagement.
- Facilitating supervision of the engagement.
- Documenting the procedures performed and the conclusions reached.
- Showing how engagement objectives were achieved.
- Providing evidence for quality control reviews, peer reviews, and inspections.
- Supporting communications with the auditee, senior management, the board of directors, and other parties.

In this chapter, we focus on how to construct, classify, organize, and review working papers. Through the remainder of the chapter, we refer to engagement documentation as working papers.

## The Experienced Auditor Standard

Working papers should always be sufficient to allow an experienced auditor to understand the nature of the work that was performed, the types of evidence obtained, and the conclusions reached by the auditor. In this context, an *experienced auditor* is one who is sufficiently competent and skilled to perform an audit, but who has no experience with the engagement in question.

## Documentation of Procedures and Evidence

The exact content of the working papers will depend on a number of factors, such as the following:

- The judgments made during the engagement
- The significance of the evidence obtained
- The size and complexity of the business unit
- The types of procedures being performed
- The types of exceptions found

The working papers may be recorded electronically or on paper. In either case, the types of documentation that should be assembled include the following:

- Engagement plans, including time budgets and resource allocations
- Agendas for auditor team meetings, as well as for meetings with the auditee
- Analyses conducted
- Any evidence compiled by the auditee and then tested by the auditor
- Questionnaires used to collect information
- Documentation of oral discussions with the auditee
- Checklists
- Auditee organization charts, job descriptions, policies and procedures
- Copies of source documents
- Evidence obtained from third parties, such as confirmations
- Flowcharts used to document processes and controls
- Memoranda and correspondence regarding the results of meetings and issues found
- Other work performed by the internal auditor that states the work performed
- Summaries of significant findings
- Management's responses to the engagement team's findings

The working papers may identify the characteristics of specific items or issues that were tested. Doing so enhances the ability of the internal audit manager to review the work performed, thereby demonstrating the accountability of the engagement team for its work, while also making it easier to investigate exceptions. Examples of the information identified include the following:

- *Systematic sampling.* List the source document being reviewed, the sampling interval, and the starting point.
- *Inquiries.* State the inquiries made, the dates when the inquiries were made, and the names and titles of the persons interviewed.
- *Observations.* State the process being observed, the individuals involved in it as well as their responsibilities, and the date and location.

It may be useful for the auditor to prepare for the working papers a completion memorandum that describes the primary issues uncovered during the engagement and how they were dealt with. Such a summary makes it easier to review the working papers, especially when it was unusually large or complex.

In the interests of keeping the working papers down to a manageable length, it is not necessary to include any of the following:

- Corrected copies
- Duplicates
- Notes regarding preliminary conclusions
- Superseded drafts

## Working Paper Preparation

A working paper should exhibit certain characteristics to ensure that it is properly identified and contains sufficient information to support its intent. The following are usually considered the key characteristics of engagement working papers:

- *Heading*. The heading on each working paper should include the name of the business unit, a description of the information being presented, and the date or period covered. The label should also indicate whether the working paper was prepared by the auditee. There should also be a unique index number to identify the working paper.
- *Scope*. The working paper should describe the scope of the work performed.
- *Description*. The working paper should adequately identify all documents examined, the sources of the data, employees interviewed, and sites visited. It should also describe the nature of all verification work performed. If tests or analyses were performed, then the details of these tests or analyses should be noted, including the methodology used to analyze data, the description of the population evaluated, and the sample size used and method of selection.
- *Commentary*. The working paper should include auditor commentary regarding the conclusions reached. This may take the form of memoranda that summarize key issues and address the judgments made and conclusions reached. Ideally, a memorandum should describe the situation that is its focus, summarize the nature of the work performed and the results obtained, and note the impact of the work on the engagement.
- *Proposed additional work*. If necessary, the working paper can state any proposed follow-up engagement work to be performed.
- *Signature*. The preparer of the working paper should date and initial the document, as should the reviewer.

During the preparation of working papers, the auditor will likely use a variety of symbols, or *tick marks*, to indicate the nature of the steps that were performed. Whenever tick marks are used, they should be accompanied by a legend that explains their meaning. For example, a tick mark could be used to indicate that a total was footed or crossfooted, or that a balance was agreed to a source document, or that a balance was confirmed with a third party, or that an authorization was examined.

Auditing software is an excellent way to create and organize working papers in an electronic format, for the following reasons:

- *Standards enforcement*. It is easier to enforce minimum working paper standards when using electronic working papers, since they require the completion of working papers in a specific format.
- *Ratio analysis*. The software can automatically conduct analytical procedures to detect anomalies.
- *Work flow*. The software can track the completion and review status of each engagement area.

Ideally, a computer-based audit can result in a nearly paperless audit.

---

**SAMPLE WORKING PAPER**

Index: **V-12**
Prepared by: Elsa Perkins
Reviewed by: Jonathan Wilcox

**Purpose of Test:** To test whether any employees are operating suppliers from which the company is buying goods or services.

**Testing Approach:** To compare the home addresses of all current employees to all supplier addresses. This is a test of 100% of all employees to 100% of all suppliers.

**Sampling Considerations:** It is possible to extract all employee records from the human resources database and all supplier records from the purchasing database. Using an electronic spreadsheet, we compared both data extracts.

**Results of Testing:** After comparing the two sets of addresses, we determined that Mr. Paul Avery, an employee in the purchasing department, owns Evergreen Lumber, from which the company has routinely acquired building supplies.

**Conclusion:** According to the purchasing department's records, Mr. Avery has issued $129,000 of purchase orders to his own company without notifying the purchasing manager of this conflict of interest. This represents an active fraud risk, which has been referred to senior management for further action. We also recommend that a conflict of interest policy be included in the employee manual, and that this same test be conducted on an annual basis.

**Proposed Additional Work:** We recommend that background checks be conducted on all employees within the purchasing department to ascertain whether they own other businesses.

---

## Working Paper Reviews

Working papers are reviewed by each successive level of supervisors within the internal audit department. Thus, senior auditors review the working papers prepared by staff auditors, while the internal audit manager reviews the working papers again. At all levels of review, working papers will likely be subjected to a more intensive level of review when they deal with what are considered riskier areas for the targeted business unit. The engagement manager is responsible for developing conclusions about the work performed, after his or her review of the working papers. These conclusions are typically documented in a memorandum, stating the objectives of the engagement and noting how the conclusion is supported by the work performed.

At the most detailed level, the review process involves checking the mathematical accuracy of a working paper, discerning whether it fully addresses the applicable section of the engagement program, checking whether it is properly cross-referenced, and deciding whether the conclusions reached are reasonable and supported by the evidence.

In general, reviewers want to determine whether a set of working papers properly document an engagement. The more technical reviews are conducted lower in the department's hierarchy, to ensure that procedures have been completed properly, and that the associated findings and conclusions were clearly expressed. The reviews by individuals higher in the department are more concerned with whether the audit was performed in accordance with IIA standards. These latter reviews are typically conducted for all working papers at once, in order to see if the working papers support each other, and to see if there are any inconsistencies or omissions that should be corrected.

## Working Paper Best Practices

The internal auditor may spend an inordinate amount of time preparing and reviewing working papers. To reduce the work load, consider using the following best practices:

- *Discuss standards in advance*. The engagement manager should meet with all staff assigned to an engagement and clearly state his or her standards for how the working papers should be prepared, possibly including examples of what he or she considers to be both well-prepared and poor working papers. Doing so can result in a noticeable reduction in the volume of review notes sent back to members of the audit team that need to be cleared.
- *Use engagement program instead*. The engagement program may contain a sufficient amount of detail regarding required inspections and verifications that the program can take the place of working papers that essentially say the same thing. However, if exceptions are noted, they must be discussed in a separate memorandum. In short, this approach is most efficient when no exceptions are expected or found.
- *Self-review working papers*. The person preparing working papers would be well advised to set them aside for a short period of time following their completion, and then review them for errors and omissions. Doing so will keep the reviewer from finding these problems, which not only reduces the reviewer's effort, but also improves the reputation of the preparer.
- *Review as soon as possible*. The engagement manager should review working papers as soon as they have been completed by subordinates. By doing so and issuing review notes right away, the matters discussed in the working papers are still fresh in the minds of the staff, who can therefore clear the review notes more promptly. In addition, it is much more efficient for the staff to clear review notes when they are still on-site at the business unit, rather than back at the office.
- *Use standard indexing format*. Use the same indexing system across all engagements, thereby making it easier to peruse working papers, no matter what the engagement may be.
- *Search for unreferenced working papers*. The entire package of working papers is considered a coherent argument that has been compiled to support the engagement team's conclusions. This means that every document in the

package should be cross-referenced in some way to support that argument. A high degree of cross-referencing also makes it easier for a reviewer to follow the logical flow of a supporting argument through the working papers.

- *Enforce department-wide tick marks.* The tick marks used by an internal audit department should be consistently applied across the working papers for all engagements. Doing so minimizes the risk that a reviewer will mistakenly assume that a certain procedure had been performed, when that was not really the case.
- *Improve legibility.* One of the better reasons for using auditing software is simply to improve the legibility of the working papers. The use of software eliminates written scrawls that are indecipherable or at least subject to misunderstanding.
- *Standardize permanent file inclusions.* Identify the types of information that should be stored in a permanent file for each auditee, which can then be easily extracted for use in future audits of that auditee.

## Summary

This chapter addressed the requirements for what needs to be included in audit working papers, and then went on to cover how they should be constructed, classified, organized, and reviewed. We also noted a number of best practices to enhance the efficiency of the working paper creation and review process, which can lead to a reduction in overall engagement costs. In total, the topics covered here can assist the auditor in dealing with one of the core underlying issues in an internal audit engagement – the paperwork.

# Chapter 11
# Audit Sampling

## Introduction

The massive amounts of data generated by auditees make it quite difficult for internal auditors to examine 100% of all records, unless data analytics tools are used (see the next chapter). For the many cases to which data analytics cannot be applied, the most efficient alternative is audit sampling. *Audit sampling* is the use of an audit procedure to select and evaluate less than 100% of a population, in order to draw inferences about the population. There are multiple ways to engage in audit sampling, including the use of block sampling, haphazard sampling, random sampling, and systematic sampling, all of which are covered in the following pages.

This chapter is intended to assist internal auditors in understanding the situations in which audit sampling can be applied, and how to do so.

> **Note:** There is a declining need for internal auditors to use audit sampling, because data analytics can be used to analyze 100% of the population in many cases.

## Statistical and Nonstatistical Sampling

The internal auditor can choose to use either statistical sampling or nonstatistical sampling. Statistical sampling involves the random selection of sample items and the use of probability theory to evaluate sample results. Conversely, nonstatistical sampling involves the selection of a test group that is based on the auditor's judgment, rather than a formal statistical method. Either approach can provide sufficient appropriate audit evidence. Of the two, statistical sampling is more theoretically correct. It can help to identify the minimum amount of evidence that must be obtained, and helps the auditor to quantitatively evaluate the results of the test. In addition, statistical sampling helps the auditor to quantify and control sampling risk. However, it can be more costly to conduct, because the auditor needs to be properly trained in its use and needs to spend more time designing and selecting samples.

If a sampling procedure does not allow for the numerical measurement of sampling risk, then it is considered a nonstatistical sampling procedure. This does not mean that a properly designed nonstatistical sampling procedure cannot provide equally effective results, only that it cannot explicitly measure sampling risk.

There is a risk that an auditor's judgment in developing a sample size for a nonstatistical sample will be quite different from the size calculated for a statistical sample. Accordingly, some internal audit departments develop nonstatistical sampling guides for their staff, which allows for a higher degree of consistency across their engagements.

## Audit Risk and Sampling Risk

There is some uncertainty arising from the use of sampling, since it is possible that the results will cause the auditor to reach an invalid conclusion, which is known as *audit risk*. The uncertainties related to audit risk encompass sampling risk and nonsampling risk. They are as follows:

- *Sampling risk*. This is the possibility that the items selected in a sample are not truly representative of the population being tested. As the sample size increases as a proportion of the total population, sampling risk declines. Conversely, a small sample size has a higher sampling risk.
- *Nonsampling risk*. This is the risk of reaching an erroneous conclusion for any reason other than something related to sampling risk. Or, stated differently, nonsampling risk is the probability of arriving at an incorrect conclusion, despite having selected a correct sample. Under these circumstances, even 100% testing of an entire population would not be effective. Nonsampling risk can be reduced by engaging in an appropriate amount of engagement work planning and supervision, as well as by using an effective quality control system.

---

**Tip:** When the internal auditor has a choice of auditing procedures, both of which provide the same level of assurance and at the same approximate cost, one would typically select the procedure having the lower nonsampling risk.

---

When conducting tests of controls, the auditor needs to be concerned about two characteristics of sampling risk, which are:

- *Risk of over-reliance*. This is the risk that the auditor will incorrectly conclude that a control is more effective than is really the case, which can lead to excessive reliance on that control.
- *Risk of under-reliance*. This is the risk that the auditor will incorrectly conclude that a control is less effective than is really the case, which can lead to an incorrectly reduced reliance on that control.

These risks of over-reliance and under-reliance on a control impact *control risk*, which is the risk that the system of controls fails to reduce controllable risk to an acceptable level. *Controllable risk* is that portion of the inherent risk of a business that can be reduced through the proper management of day-to-day operations. Controls are specifically intended to reduce controllable risk, ideally to a level at or below management's tolerance for risk. If the remaining amount of risk after controls have been implemented is higher than management's tolerance for risk, then the system of controls is considered to be ineffective.

## Tests of Controls Using Statistical Audit Sampling

There are several sampling approaches available for the auditor who elects to apply audit sampling to tests of controls. The first of these plans is *attribute sampling*, which involves the selection of a small number of transactions and making assumptions about how their characteristics represent the full population of which the selected items are a part. The concept is used to test a population for certain characteristics, such as the presence of an authorizing signature or approval stamp on a document. The concept can be used to determine whether various controls are functioning in a reliable manner. The result of attribute sampling is binary – either a condition exists or it does not exist. Thus, there is no gray area in attribute sampling. Also, equal weight is given to each occurrence or deviation from a control, no matter what the dollar amount of each transaction may be. Examples of typical attribute sampling tests are:

- 50 out of 60 invoices were supported by a sales order.
- 38 out of 40 supplier invoices that were greater than $1,000 contained an approval signature.
- 19 out of 20 fixed asset purchases had a supporting authorization document signed by the company president.
- Three out of 80 invoices are overdue for payment.
- The early payment discount was not taken on two out of 11 supplier invoices.
- 13 out of 211 journal entries were posted to the wrong account.

The results of an attribute sampling test are then compared to the tolerable error rate established for that test. If the test results are worse than the tolerable error rate, the control point related to the test has failed, and should be revised or replaced. When the tested sampling rate falls just outside the acceptable error rate, it is possible that conducting more tests with a larger sample size will result in an actual error rate that falls within the acceptable error rate. Thus, the first reaction to a marginal attribute sampling result is to keep on testing with a larger sample group. This expansion of the sample size frequently does not yield a better result, as the original smaller sample size already provided the correct insight into the underlying error rate.

An alternative approach is *sequential sampling* (also known as stop-or-go sampling), which involves the evaluation of each sample taken from a population to see if it fits a desired conclusion. The auditor stops evaluating samples as soon as there is sufficient support for the conclusion. If the initial evaluation does not support the conclusion, the person conducting the test incrementally increases the sample size and continues to test, trying to reach the desired outcome that supports the desired conclusion. Sequential sampling can be quite efficient, since it minimizes the amount of testing.

## Audit Sampling in Tests of Controls

In this section, we provide an overview of audit sampling as it relates to tests of controls, as well as the determination of sample size, implementing the sampling plan, and reviewing the results.

### Test Objectives

When testing controls, the objective is to collect evidence about the operating effectiveness of those controls. To do so, the auditor needs to address whether the controls were performed, how they were performed, and who performed them.

The use of audit sampling for tests of controls is most appropriate when the designated controls leave behind documentary evidence after they were completed. When there is no documentary evidence, the auditor might still be able to plan relevant audit procedures by observing the controls in action. If so, sampling can involve designating certain dates, times, and locations where the controls will be observed. If observation is to be performed, this approach will need to be planned for early in the engagement, to ensure that all observations can be completed by the end of the engagement.

### Deviation Conditions

The auditor will need to identify those characteristics that are indicative of the proper performance of a control, and then define the associated deviation conditions. A *deviation* is a departure from the expected performance of a targeted control. Performance occurs when every step associated with a control has been completed. For example, the three-way matching control requires that a clerk (1) match the supplier invoice to the authorizing purchase order, (2) match the supplier invoice to receiving documentation, and (3) flag error conditions. For this control, an error could be defined as not flagging error conditions, even if the first two control activities are completed.

### Population

The population is the entire set of data from which a sample is selected. The auditor needs to determine the population that is most appropriate to meet the audit objective, since the results of an audit sample can only be projected for the population from which the sample was derived. For example, to test the operating effectiveness of a control that is supposed to ensure that only authorized purchases are paid for, it would be reasonable to sample the population of received goods to determine whether selected deliveries were paid for.

When dealing with a population, a possible concern is whether the physical representation of the population actually includes the entire population. For example, if the auditor wants to perform a test of controls for all billings issued to customers in the past year, those billings are considered to be the population. If the auditor physically selects the billings from a filing cabinet, the billings stored within that cabinet are the physical representation of the population. If some of the billings have been removed from the filing cabinet, then any conclusions reached by the auditor only apply to the invoices actually stored in the filing cabinet. This is less of a problem when the source is controlled, so that there are minimal differences between the physical representation of the population and the actual population. In our example, this could be achieved by making selections from a billings register for which the auditor has tested the total, so that the auditor has reasonable assurance that the register contains the same transactions as the population. In any cases in which the physical representation has missing items, the auditor should certainly make inquiries about the reason for the difference.

## Sampling Unit

For the purposes of sampling for tests of controls, a sampling unit is anything for which its examination results in evidence of how the control operates. This may, for example, be a document containing evidence of a review with an approval signature. Each sampling unit comprises one item within the designated population. It is possible that one sampling unit will provide evidence concerning the application of more than one control. For example, a review of shipping documentation might indicate not only that the ordered goods were shipped, but also that the order was previously approved by the credit department.

From the standpoint of efficiency, it is generally best to define a sampling unit as narrowly as possible, since doing so reduces the amount of associated audit work. For example, if the auditor has the choice of defining an entire supplier invoice as the sampling unit or a specific line item on that invoice, efficiency dictates defining the sampling unit as just the line item. Otherwise, the auditor will have to examine every line item on the invoice, which could involve substantially more work.

## Method of Sample Selection

When selecting a sample, the items chosen should be representative of the population, so that the results of the sample can be extrapolated to the population. This overall objective has the following ramifications:

- All items in the population should have an opportunity to be selected.
- For statistical sampling, use a random sampling method to select the sample.
- For nonstatistical sampling, use a selection method that approximates a random sampling approach.

Selection methods that may be used include the following:

- *Simple random sampling.* This is an approach where every combination of sampling units has the same probability of being selected, so that the result is a statistically unbiased sample. To follow this approach, one can match randomly-generated numbers to document numbers, thereby performing a selection. In this case, sampling risk still exists, because there is always a possibility that a sample will be selected that does not possess the same characteristics as the population. It can be used for both statistical and nonstatistical sampling. Techniques used to select random samples include the following:

o *Random number tables*. Random number tables are widely available, and provide (as the name implies) a set of randomly-generated numbers. Such a table is usually laid out in a pattern of rows and columns, which are useful for easily selecting numbers. A sample random number table appears in the following exhibit. To use a random number table, establish a linkage between the digits in the table and the items in the population, which is most easily achieved when the items in the population have been consecutively numbered. When consecutive numbering is not present, the auditor will need to renumber the population. Next, the auditor selects a starting point and a systematic method for reading the random number table; any method is acceptable, as long as it is followed consistently. For example, an auditee's trade receivables are numbered from 1 to 8,000 and the auditor wants to select a random sample of 80 invoices for confirmation. Using the following table, the auditor decides to start at the top of Column C and proceed from top to bottom. Reading only the first four digits of the numbers in Column C, the auditor would select 6911, 7563, and 4079 as three of the invoice numbers to be included in her sample. Further down in the column, number 8311 would be ignored, since there is no population item with that number.

**Random Number Table**

| Row | A | B | C | D | E |
|---|---|---|---|---|---|
| 1 | 36518 | 36777 | 69116 | 05542 | 29705 |
| 2 | 46132 | 81380 | 75635 | 19428 | 88048 |
| 3 | 31841 | 77367 | 40791 | 97402 | 27569 |
| 4 | 84180 | 93793 | 64953 | 51472 | 65358 |
| 5 | 78435 | 37586 | 07015 | 98729 | 76703 |
| 6 | 41859 | 94198 | 37182 | 61345 | 88857 |
| 7 | 13019 | 07274 | 51068 | 93129 | 40386 |
| 8 | 82448 | 72430 | 29041 | 59208 | 95266 |
| 9 | 25432 | 96593 | 83112 | 96997 | 55340 |
| 10 | 69226 | 38655 | 03811 | 08342 | 47863 |

When using a random number table, it is possible that the auditor will encounter the same number more than once. If she ignores all subsequent encounters with the same number and moves on to the next number, this is considered to be sampling without replacement, which means that once an item has been selected, it cannot be selected again. The alternative is sampling *with* replacement, where an item that has been selected for review can subsequently be examined again as part of the same sample. From a practical perspective, auditors most commonly employ sampling without replacement, which avoids questions about the propriety of including an item more than once in a sample.

- o *Random number generators*. When a random number table is used to select a large sample, the selection process can be rather lengthy. An alternative that shortens this process is a random number generator, which is available as a computer program (such as Excel). Such a generator can produce a list of random numbers of any needed length, which can then be applied to a population.

- *Systematic sampling*. This is an approach where one can use a rational technique for picking a sample, typically by dividing the number of units in the population by the sample size. For example, one could begin sampling at a random point in the population, and then make additional selections at a predetermined interval. Thus, if the decision is made to review 100 invoices in a population of 10,000 invoices, a systematic sampling approach would be to select every 100th invoice. Accordingly, the auditor randomly decides to pick the 57th invoice (sorted by invoice number), followed by the 157th invoice, 257th invoice, 357th invoice, and so on. This approach can be inefficient, but ensures that a broad sample is selected that is likely to be relatively representative of the entire population. However, the sample may not be representative of the population if the list from which the sample was selected is organized in such a manner that the selections are not entirely random. Systematic sampling can be used for both statistical and nonstatistical sampling, depending on the population bias issue just noted.
- *Haphazard sampling*. This is an approach that is nonstatistical in nature, but which attempts to approximate a random selection by making selections without any conscious bias, which the auditor intends to be representative of the population. It can be difficult for bias not to enter into this type of selection, since an auditor may be tempted to select items that are more convenient, or to engage in block sampling (see next). Consequently, this approach is only used for nonstatistical sampling.
- *Block sampling*. This is an approach where a sequential series of selections is made. For example, an auditor elects to use block sampling to examine customer invoices, and intends to pick 50 invoices. She picks invoice numbers 1000 through 1049. This approach is very efficient, since a large cluster of documents can be pulled from one location. However, a more random selection method would do a better job of sampling the entire population. When using block sampling, sampling risk can be reduced by selecting a large number of blocks of samples.

## Sample Size

When performing tests of controls, the auditor is concerned with forming an erroneous conclusion that the controls are more effective than is really the case, and (alternatively) reaching a conclusion that the controls are less effective than is really the case.

To lower the acceptable risk that a control is more effective than is really the case, one should increase the sample size. However, the auditor may elect to keep the sample size at a lower level when other evidence (such as a redundant control) is also available. A common reason for relying on other evidence is when there are highly effective and well-documented tests of those same controls, upon which the auditor chooses to rely.

When controls are associated with populations of unusual transactions, as well as complex revenue recognition situations, an auditor may consider increasing the sample sizes of the related tests of controls. Doing so reduces the risk of reaching an incorrect conclusion regarding the effectiveness of these controls.

## Tolerable Rate of Deviation

The *tolerable rate of deviation* is the largest percentage variance experienced in audit sampling that an auditor will accept, while still concluding that the control is acceptably effective. If the deviation rate is higher than this threshold value, then the auditor cannot conclude that the control is effective.

One's judgment about the level of the tolerable rate of deviation is derived from the relative importance of the control being tested. Thus, when a control is considered to be essential, the auditor should set a low tolerable deviation rate. A higher rate may be used when a control is considered to be less essential.

## Effect of Population Size

The determination of sample size is not impacted significantly by the size of the associated population, except when the population is quite small. Generally, the population needs to be comprised of fewer than 200 items for there to be a significant reduction in the sample size.

Some controls are only used by the auditee at relatively long intervals, such as during a semi-weekly payroll or during the month-end close. These controls may be of some importance, because they are linked to processes that involve substantial amounts of funds. The sample size for these low-volume controls will typically require two items when a control operates once a quarter (so half of the population is being sampled), while the sample size will likely require between five and nine items when a control operates once a week (so 10% to 17% of the population is being sampled).

## Sampling Plan Performance

Once a sampling plan has been written, the auditor selects a sample from the designated population and examines the selected items to see if there are any deviations from the targeted control. At this stage, it can make sense to select a few extra items as part of the sample. By doing so, the auditor already has access to additional items if it becomes necessary to expand the sample size. When this happens, the auditor should examine the extra sample items in the same order in which the underlying random numbers were generated.

It is possible that an audit sample will contain a voided item. If so, and the item was properly voided and does not represent a deviation from the control that is under review, then the auditor should replace the voided item with another selection. The same treatment applies when an unused or inapplicable document is included in a sample. This situation can also arise when the size of the population was overestimated, resulting in selections of items that do not yet exist; when this happens, any items selected that do not yet exist are treated as unused documents, so they are replaced.

There may be cases in which a document that is a designated item within a sample cannot be found. If so, the auditor should consider the following options:

1. Whether there are any alternatives that can be used to substitute for the missing document.
2. If the first option is not available, treat the missing document as a deviation for the purpose of evaluating the sample.
3. In addition to the second step, consider the reasons for the missing document, and how those reasons might impact the auditee's control risk and audit risk. For example, if a missing purchase order could be an indicator of fraud, then the auditor may need to devise an audit response to address the issue.

## Reaching a Conclusion

Once the internal auditor has completed the sampling process, including a summary of all deviations from designated controls, it is time to evaluate the results. One of the first steps in this process is to calculate the deviation rate. This is accomplished by dividing the number of observed deviations by the sample size. The resulting deviation rate is the auditor's best estimate of the deviation rate for the entire population.

The auditor should investigate any systematic causes that are identified. This step may include the identification of all items in the population that share a common feature, followed by a detailed investigation of each one. This more penetrating approach to systematic causes may identify instances of ongoing fraud.

## Sequential Sampling

When setting up a sampling plan, the auditor has a choice of doing so with either a fixed or sequential sampling plan. Thus far, we have mostly mentioned the fixed sampling plan approach, where a sample of a specific size is developed and investigated. Under a *sequential sampling plan*, a sample is instead selected in several steps, with the actions taken in each successive step being contingent on the results observed in the prior steps. This approach can result in fewer sampling units being examined, though the sampling will continue if any deviations are found. Consequently, sequential sampling plans work best when few deviations are expected.

A sequential sample is usually comprised of anywhere from two to four groups of sampling units. The auditor uses a computer program to determine the size of each of these groups, based on the tolerable rate of deviation, the risk of overreliance, and the expected rate of population deviation.

The sequential sampling process begins with the auditor examining the first group of sampling units. Based on the results of this examination, the auditor decides whether to:

1.  Accept the assessed level of control risk, without engaging in any additional sampling;
2.  Halt any further sampling, because the tolerable rate of deviation cannot be achieved due to the presence of too many deviations; or
3.  Engage in the examination of additional sampling units in order to gather more information about whether the planned assessed level of control risk can be supported.

For example, an auditor develops a set of three groups of sampling units, where each successive group contains the same number of units to be sampled. The sampling plan is to continue to the next group of sampling units if the preceding group contains at least one deviation. Several outcomes are:

*   *Scenario 1.* An analysis of the first group uncovers no deviations, so the auditor concludes that the sample supports the planned assessed level of control risk. Accordingly, she decides not to examine any additional sampling units.
*   *Scenario 2.* An analysis of the first group uncovers two deviations, so the auditor decides to continue with the sampling, using the next sampling group. This second group is found to contain one additional deviation, so the audit continues to the third group of samples in her continuing quest for more information, to see if the increased sample results will eventually support the assessed level of control risk.
*   *Scenario 3.* An analysis of the first group uncovers four deviations, which is too many deviations. Engaging in the examination of further groups of sampling units will not improve the situation, so the auditor stops the sampling process.

When it appears necessary to proceed to the next group of sampling units, the auditor should consider the cost-benefit of continuing to engage in testing. It is possible that the auditor will not be willing to proceed through every group of sampling units, and instead will accept the conclusion that the tolerable rate of deviation cannot be achieved.

A risk when using sequential sampling is that the next group to be added for sampling could uncover fewer deviations than would be representative of the population, which would increase the risk of incorrect acceptance.

## Summary

In this chapter, we have described the audit sampling process and how it can be applied to tests of controls. Audit sampling is an excellent tool for deriving conclusions about a population, without actually examining every item within that population. The extensive use of sampling can greatly reduce the time required to complete a controls audit, with a high level of assurance that the conclusions reached were valid. However, doing so requires proper consideration of the concepts discussed within this chapter, to ensure that a variety of risks are incorporated into the decisions regarding sample size and the evaluation of sample results.

# Chapter 12
# Data Analytics

## Introduction

*Data analytics* is the science of analyzing raw data in order to reach a conclusion about that data. Data analytics techniques can reveal trends and metrics that would otherwise be lost in the mass of auditee data. The concept is especially useful in internal auditing, where it can be used to analyze patterns in auditee data and identify anomalies. The benefits to be derived from using data analytics in an audit include the following:

- *Improved understanding of the auditee.* Data analytics can be used to develop an enhanced risk profile for an auditee, which may result in a revised allocation of time to various audit procedures. Analytics may also allow the internal auditor to detect the areas in which fraud is more likely to be present.
- *Improved detection of misstatements.* Data analytics can be used to examine 100% of a large data set, which reduces the need for sampling, which in turn minimizes sampling risk[2].
- *Improved communications.* The use of data analytics can provide the auditor with deeper insights into auditee matters that may be of interest to those charged with governance, who can use this information to better oversee operations.

In short, the use of data analytics provides an opportunity to enhance the quality of an internal audit engagement, especially in environments where the auditee has amassed large amounts of data that can be sifted with data analytics tools. This chapter describes how data analytics can be employed within an engagement, with specific usage examples.

## Potential Uses of Data Analytics

There are many uses of data analytics within the field of internal auditing. The exact choices made will vary by business unit, depending on the amount of data that is collected, the format in which it is stored, and the demands placed on the auditor. Nonetheless, these uses are likely to fall within the following four areas:

- *Fraud detection.* An excellent use is fraud detection, where data analytics can examine 100% of the data in a population to pinpoint fake employees, asset

---

[2] Sampling risk is the possibility that the items selected in a sample are not truly representative of the population being tested.

misappropriations, employees who also own suppliers, purchases being made just under the authorization threshold, and so forth.

- *Controls.* It can provide warnings of control breaches and weaknesses, such as inappropriate employee access to certain databases, notations on outlier events indicating control breaches, and areas in which duties need to be segregated.
- *Compliance.* It can be used to evaluate how well employees and business partners are complying with the business unit's policies, procedures, and controls. Thus, it could be used to examine the mass of data associated with freight bills, to determine whether the firm has been charged the correct rates. Or, it could be used internally to examine procurement card purchases to see if employees have been using these cards correctly.
- *Operational performance.* It can uncover any number of performance issues throughout the operations of a business unit, such as specific slow-moving items within the warehouse, payables that are being paid too early, perennial late-paying customers, excessive scrap levels in production, and so forth.

## Considerations When Selecting A Data Analytics Procedure

When considering which data analytics procedure to employ, one should first run through a number of considerations that may have a bearing on the decision. They are as follows:

- *The question to be answered.* The method chosen could depend on the objective to be achieved and the value to derived from it. For example, an investigation of fraud could point toward the use of analytics that sift through 100% of a population of suspect transactions.
- *The nature of usage.* The choice made may vary, based on the size of the account balances being tested, the nature of these accounts, and the types of transactions being tested.
- *The persuasiveness of the evidence.* The method chosen could depend on the level of persuasiveness needed for the evidence.
- *The combinations of targeted tasks.* The method selected could depend on the combination of tasks being contemplated by the auditor, such as searching for data with specific attributes, while at the same time determining whether there are any correlations among variables.

## Data Access Concerns

One of the principal concerns with using data analytics is the great variety of ways in which data may be stored by auditees. It may be stored on different types of data storage devices, and may be stored in any number of formats. These problems may be worsened by the presence of different systems within the same business unit, especially when there is a separate system operating in each department, with little interoperability across the entity. These concerns are reduced if the software has a data export function that can convert it into a format usable by the auditor's audit software. Nonetheless, there is no data formatting standard, so using auditee data will probably continue to be a challenge.

Even if the data can be accessed, it is quite possible that a considerable amount of scrubbing will need to be completed before the data can be analyzed. *Data scrubbing* involves removing or modifying data that are incomplete, incorrect, improperly formatted, or duplicated. After the scrubbing process is complete, data should be able to meet the following criteria:

- *Validity*. This is the degree to which the data conform to defined business rules or constraints. This is generally not a problem when the auditee is using modern database technology, but can arise when it uses data-capture technology where it is difficult to limit what is entered into a field (such as spreadsheets). Data constraints are usually classified as follows:

    o *Cross-field validation*. Where the values in one field are used as conditions that must be met by the values in another field. For example, an invoice date cannot be earlier than the ship date for the related product.
    o *Data-type*. Where the data must be of a particular data type, such as numeric, alphabetic, or date.
    o *Mandatory*. Where an entry must be made into a field.
    o *Range*. Where numbers or dates should fall within a predetermined set of high and low values.
    o *Regular expression pattern*. Where data must be entered in a certain manner, such as a phone number that must include a hyphen after the third and sixth digits.
    o *Set-membership*. Where the available values for a field come from a set of discrete values, such as a State field that can only be filled from a drop-down menu of two-digit state name contractions.
    o *Unique*. Where an entry in a field cannot be duplicated across a dataset, such as an invoice number.

- *Completeness*. This is the degree to which all required data are known. It can be very difficult to fill in incomplete or empty fields through the data scrubbing process, so a low degree of completeness may make it impossible to proceed with data analytics activities.
- *Consistency*. This is the degree to which a set of data is equivalent across multiple files. Inconsistency arises when two data items in a data set contradict each other. For example, a supplier record drawn from two different systems contains conflicting mailing addresses.
- *Uniformity*. This is the degree to which data are specified using the same units of measure. For example, the inventory records from an auditee business unit may list an inventory item in rolls, while the same inventory item kept by a different business unit is recorded in inches.

The data scrubbing process can render the use of data analytics not cost-effective, depending on the complexity of the scrubbing steps needed. At a minimum, a difficult data scrubbing process will suggest to the auditor that the auditee does not have effective controls over its data.

## Identification of Many Exceptions

A significant scenario arising from the use of data analytics to examine a large population is that the process will uncover quite a few items that appear to require further investigation. Some of these items may turn out to be *false positives*, while others may relate to a previously unidentified risk or perhaps greater control deficiencies than the auditor had initially assessed. In deciding whether the items found warrant a response, one might consider the following:

- Reapply the data analytics, using more clearly defined data characteristics. Doing so may eliminate extraneous data items that do not require an audit response.
- Break down the population into subgroups, and then perform additional data analytics procedures that are unique to each subgroup. Doing so may result in conclusions that certain subgroups do not pose a risk of control deficiencies. Conversely, the additional procedures may indicate more clearly which subgroups *do* require further investigation.
- Apply different data analytics that may more clearly identify those data items that pose a risk of control deficiencies.

## Data Analytics Documentation

When conducting data analytics, the internal auditor should include the following in the related documentation:

- The scope and objectives of the procedure.
- The risks of control deficiencies that the procedure was intended to investigate.
- The nature of the population that was analyzed, including its source(s) and the reason it was selected.
- The type of data analytics used, as well as screen shots of any visualizations generated that support the auditor's work.
- The process used to group and filter items when a large number of items are identified that call for further investigation.
- How the data was accessed and transformed for audit use.
- The investigation of any issues identified as a result of the procedure, and any actions taken.
- The nature of all non-trivial misstatements identified as a result of the procedure.

It will probably not be possible to include all the data analyzed in the audit documentation.

## Conducting a Data Analytics Procedure

The following steps should be followed to plan for, conduct, and evaluate a data analytics procedure, where the intent is either to identify and assess risks of control deficiencies:

1. *Plan the procedure.* Determine the uses to which the procedure will be put, as well as the extent of the population to which it will be applied. Also, select the analytics techniques and tools that will be best suited to the intended purpose and objectives. The objectives may be impacted by the nature of the auditee, such as the industry within which it operates, its operations, its strategies and related business risks, and its internal controls.
2. *Access and prepare the associated data.* Obtain access to the data, convert it into a readable format, engage in data scrubbing as needed, and load it into the data analytics software.
3. *Perform the procedure.* If the procedure uncovers issues that warrant further action, plan and perform procedures on these issues. If the initial results of the procedure indicate that it requires revision, then make the necessary changes and reiterate the process, changing any data groupings and employing data filtering as needed.
4. *Evaluate the results.* Decide whether the objectives of the procedure have been achieved. If not, plan for and perform alternative procedures that are more likely to achieve the objectives.

The performance of a data analytics procedure may result in the identification of a *notable item*, which is an item spotted within a population that may be indicative of a risk of reaching an incorrect conclusion that had either not been previously assessed or which is higher than originally assessed. Or, the item may provide information that can be used to design procedures to address additional issues. When only a small number of notable items have been found, the auditor may be able to conduct a manual review of these items to determine their cause.

In other cases, a data analytics procedure may uncover a larger number of notable items that cannot be easily addressed manually. In this case, the auditor should first consider whether the procedure was conducted correctly. If not, the procedure should be adjusted and conducted again. If the procedure *was* conducted correctly, then the auditor may need to engage in a process of grouping and filtering, where the notable items are reviewed using additional data analytics to weed out false positives, leaving a smaller number of items that require a manual review. Several iterations of data analytics procedures may be required to arrive at a group of notable items that can then be examined manually, and in detail.

---

**EXAMPLE**

An internal auditor has used data analytics to identify and assess risks of misstatement related to the adequacy of an auditee's reserve for obsolete inventory. The auditor develops a model that includes the historical demand for finished goods, how long since products have been on the market, the usage history of raw materials, and the number of engineering change orders that have been issued in the past.

The initial performance of the procedure uncovers a large number of notable items, which had characteristics indicating that they would not be sold in a timely manner, thereby increasing the risk of both raw material and finished goods obsolescence. A further review indicates that there is a strong after-market for the disposal of many of these items at their cost, which renders these items irrelevant in relation to the objective of the procedure. Accordingly, the auditor redesigns the analytics model to exclude any inventory items that can be sold on the after-market for at least their cost. This results in a significant reduction in the number of notable items. This brings the quantity of notable items down to a level at which the auditor can investigate further, and in more detail.

For example, the auditor goes on to break the notable items down into separate groups, which identifies a cluster of raw material items that are no longer being used, because the imposition of several engineering change orders has resulted in no further use for them.

---

## Case Study – Account Balances

An internal auditor wants to assess the risk of misstatements in an auditee's beginning account balances. To this end, she wants to search for unusual trends from prior years, which can then be used to decide whether any changes are needed to other risk assessment procedures. To form her expectations for what would be considered an unusual variance, she relies on information garnered during prior year engagements, as well as initial discussions with management regarding any changes to the business unit during the current year. Based on these expectations, she decides that a change of $100,000 from the prior year would warrant further investigation.

In addition, the auditor decides to calculate several ratios that are relevant to the financial condition and financial position of the auditee, which can then be used to identify possible areas of higher risk of misstatement. The ratios she decides to use are as follows:

Liquidity Ratios

- Current ratio
- Days sales in receivables

Margin Ratios

- Gross margin ratio
- EBITDA ratio
- Net profit ratio

The auditor uses audit software to access the auditee's account data for the past three years, as well as its current-year account data, which then calculates the dollar and percentage changes in accounts, as well as the indicated ratios for each year. A side benefit of using audit software is that the auditor can access the transaction details for any accounts that appear to require additional investigation, thereby increasing her efficiency. The analysis of changes from the prior year appears in the following exhibit.

**Account Changes**

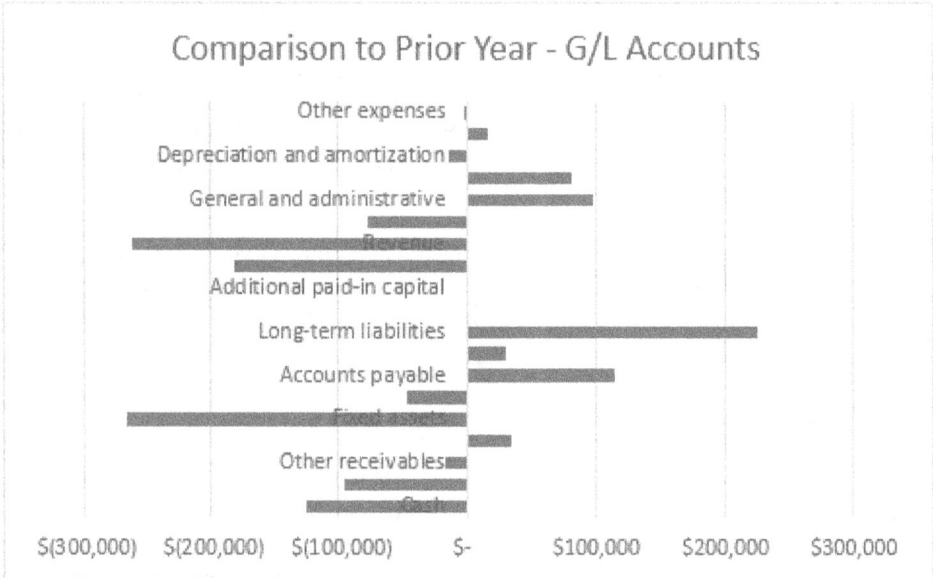

Comparison to Prior Year - G/L Accounts

In the preceding exhibit, the form of presentation makes it easy to see which accounts have changed by more than $100,000 from the prior year, such as cash, fixed assets, and long-term liabilities, which suggest areas of further investigation for the auditor.

The software also produced two charts containing ratios based on the auditee's account data for the past four years, which appear in the following two exhibits. The charts reveal a definite trend toward reduced financial performance and financial position. The auditee has consistently generated worsening margin ratios of all types, while also experiencing increased liquidity issues. These trends indicate a heightened risk of misstatements in some accounts.

## Liquidity Ratio Analysis

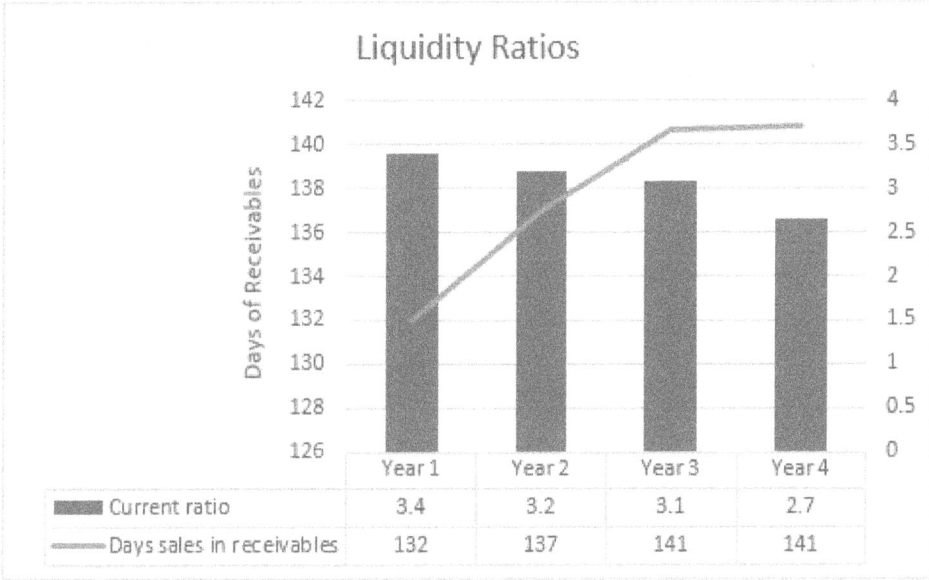

| | Year 1 | Year 2 | Year 3 | Year 4 |
|---|---|---|---|---|
| Current ratio | 3.4 | 3.2 | 3.1 | 2.7 |
| Days sales in receivables | 132 | 137 | 141 | 141 |

## Margin Ratio Analysis

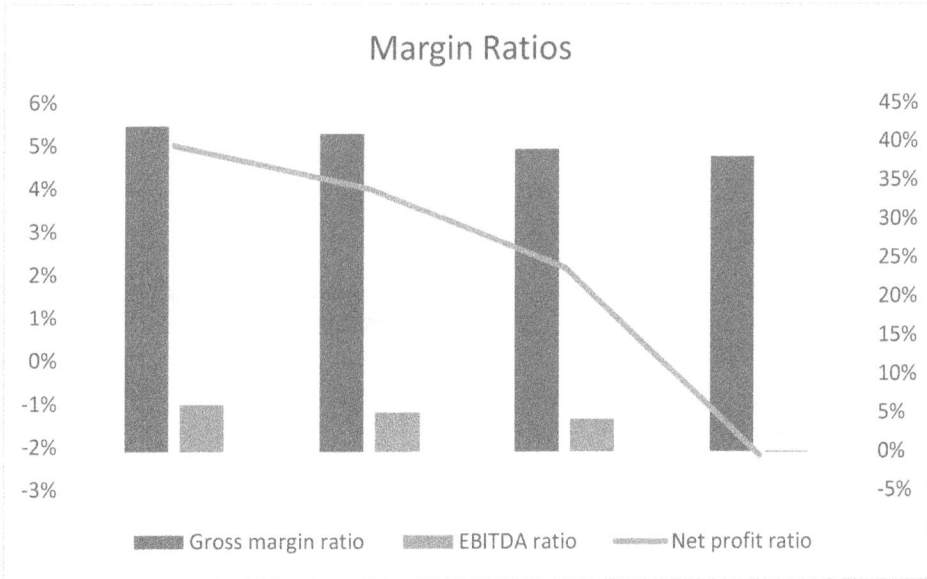

## Case Study – Discount Rates

An auditor wants to assess the risk that an auditee has incorrectly billed its customers. This business unit manufactures plumbing fixtures, which are sold to retailers. The auditee grants varying discounts to these retailers, based on the number of units sold to them. In general, the organization grants a 30% discount to its retailers, with variations of no more than 5% above and below this value, based on its stated pricing structure. To test whether this is actually the case, the auditor uses audit software to extract all billing transactions from its database for the past year, and compare the billed prices to the standard prices for each product, resulting in a calculated discount rate. The outcome appears in the following exhibit, where the red arrows highlight three instances in which billings involved either unusually high or low discounts from the standard prices. The auditor should consider investigating all three of these billings to ascertain the reasons for the unusual discounts.

**Discount Rate Analysis**

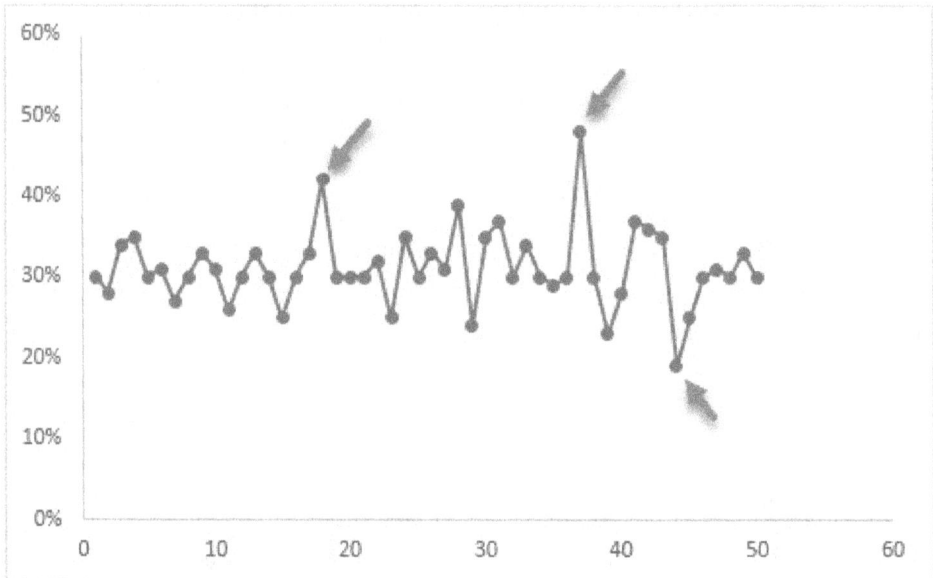

Further investigation of the billings involving the highest discount rate reveal that both were to previously unidentified related parties. With this information, the auditor concludes that there is an increased risk of other undisclosed related parties being present, and so plans to engage in additional searches for other related parties. Otherwise, the analysis is consistent with what the auditor was expecting, and so she concludes that, other than the issue associated with the related party, there is not an increased risk of misstatement.

## Case Study – Revenue Process

An auditor wants to assess how rigorously an auditee's employees are adhering to the standard procedure for processing customer orders and issuing invoices. The auditee in question uses an enterprise resources planning (ERP) system that underlies its entire distribution business, and so stores all of its transactions within a single database, from the initial recordation of a customer order through the release of orders to the warehouse for fulfillment, and the preparation of customer invoices. The ERP tracks the identification of every person who enters transactions into the system, and associates a time stamp with each transaction. The auditor is interested not only in the intrusion of unauthorized personnel into the process, but also the existence of any *variant process paths*, where a non-standard process flow is followed. As a result of this analysis, she wants to determine whether there is an increased risk of misstatement.

The analysis is performed, and the auditor detects the following situations:

- Three orders were never sent to the credit department for approval, and instead were routed directly to the warehouse for fulfillment.
- Two orders were entered into the system by the same person who fulfilled the orders and then billed the orders.
- Four downward pricing adjustments were made by unauthorized personnel.

These findings reveal clear problems with the auditee's segregation of duties, as well as the presence of a variant process path that ignores the standard credit check on customer orders. In response to these findings, the auditor plans additional procedures to investigate the segregation of duties further, as well as to search for other unauthorized transactions by the individuals responsible for the unauthorized pricing adjustments.

## Summary

Data analytics can be an exceedingly useful tool for delving deep into an auditee's records, resulting in the identification of anomalies and trends that can be investigated further. It can also provide direct audit evidence that supplants or supplements other types of audit evidence, sometimes at a lower cost. However, data analysis will only be cost-effective if relevant data is accessible and is considered sufficiently reliable. Nonetheless, there are significant advantages associated with this audit tool, so one should be on the lookout for any situations to which it can be applied.

# Chapter 13
## Conducting Internal Audit Engagements

### Introduction

For an internal audit department to operate effectively, it needs to have a regimented process for planning and performing engagements, as well as for communicating the results of this work. In this chapter, we cover the fundamentals of the assurance engagement process, as well as multiple related topics and the essentials of the consulting engagement.

### Types of Internal Audit Engagements

The conduct of an internal audit engagement varies, depending on its type. There are two main classification of engagements, which are assurance services and consulting services. Assurance services require auditors to provide an independent assessment regarding the controls, governance, or risk management activities of a business. For example, the internal audit department might assess an organization's compliance with applicable laws and regulations pertaining to environmental issues, or it could assess the adequacy and effectiveness of the accounting department's controls over management reporting. Consulting services are agreed upon with the customer, and generally are intended to add value in the same areas, but without having the internal audit department assume any direct management responsibility. For example, the department might conduct in-house training to educate process owners about the controls for which they are responsible, or advise them about ways to streamline those processes.

### The Assurance Engagement Process

The essential steps in an assurance engagement are to plan for it, perform assurance work in accordance with the plan, and communicate the results. Or, more specifically:

- *Planning activities.* The main steps are to identify the engagement objectives and scope, understand key aspects of the auditee, spot and evaluate the design of key controls, identify and assess risks, develop a work program and test plan, and identify needed staffing requirements. A structured planning process is needed to ensure that an engagement is performed as efficiently and effectively as possible, and achieves the desired objectives. A particular concern is identifying the boundaries of the engagement, so that the audit team is tightly focused on achieving very specific objectives. For example, an assessment of billing controls might have boundaries around it that encompass the East Coast region of the company, but not its other sales regions. Another concern is that the test plan allows for the collection of enough sufficient appropriate evidence to ensure that the engagement objectives are achieved. Yet another major concern is ensuring that enough fully-qualified auditors and specialist personnel are assigned to the engagement to ensure that it can be completed in a timely manner.

**EXAMPLE**

An internal audit team is assigned to review the system of controls relating to a business unit's treasury function. As part of its planning activities, several auditors interview the treasurer, who points out that a key objective of the function is to issue funding to suppliers promptly, so that they are sufficiently liquid to deliver goods to the business unit on a just-in-time basis. The treasurer also points out another objective, which is to maximize earnings on its available cash by centralizing it in a central investment account. By knowing these objectives, the team can design a framework for defining its engagement objectives. The auditors might also make inquiries about the treasury department's business risks, the key controls intended to mitigate those risks, and how treasury personnel are held accountable for assigned tasks.

**EXAMPLE**

An audit team is planning for a review of the controls associated with a business unit's credit department. Part of this work involves the identification and assessment of the business risks that might interfere with the attainment of the credit department's objectives. In this case, a key risk is that customer orders requiring a credit review will bypass the credit department, so that orders are shipped in the absence of a review. This is a major risk, since the business unit could incur a potentially massive bad debt if a customer fails to pay. The auditors then clarify the nature of the controls used to ensure that all customer orders are routed through the credit department, and include these controls in their audit plan.

**EXAMPLE**

An audit team determines that there is a risk of duplicate payments from a business unit's accounts payable system. The system should notify the payables clerk if an invoice number has already been entered into the system. To test if this is the case, the team's test plan includes the extraction of all payments for the preceding year from the payables database and reviewing the data for duplicate payments.

- *Performance activities.* The main steps are to gather and evaluate evidence, and formulate recommendations. This can include such activities as inspecting documents, observing operations, and making inquiries. A key output is the identification of conditions that fall below the baseline expectations noted in the audit plan, and then identifying the reason for the difference. These differences are then stated in a set of recommendations that are intended to correct any observed failures in a cost-effective manner. A particular concern is how well the audit team evaluates the results to decide whether there are any issues requiring remediation. Other findings could relate to whether key controls have been designed adequately, whether they are operating effectively, and whether the associated risks are being mitigated to an acceptable level.

---

**EXAMPLE**

An audit team investigates whether inventory stored in outlying locations is being properly recorded in a business unit's inventory tracking system. They find several exceptions in one warehouse, where transactions are routinely being recorded several days late. They recommend the use of radio-frequency bar code scanners, so that all inventory transactions are recorded in real time. This recommendation is relatively cost-effective, since it does not involve the hiring of any additional staff.

**EXAMPLE**

An audit team investigates whether a business unit is properly delegating authority to sign checks. The associated test is to compare the bank's listing of approved check signers to the current organization chart. Actual testing reveals that three people are still on the bank's list of approved signers, despite no longer being employees of the entity. Accordingly, the team recommends that the bank be contacted to adjust the approved check signer list, and suggests that this step be included in the human resources procedure for processing departed employees.

---

- *Communication activities*. The key point of this step is to provide management and the board with evidence of how effectively the firm's risks are being mitigated by its system of controls. More specifically, the internal auditor is expected to engage in preliminary communications, develop and communicate the final engagement results, and conduct subsequent follow-up procedures. A particular concern is bringing critical matters to the attention of management immediately, so that they can take corrective action at once. Another concern is that management has sufficient time to review a preliminary draft of the final report, so that they have a chance to offer a rebuttal, as well as to fully understand the findings.

These steps tend to be jumbled together, since the initial findings of the process may require re-planning in an iterative cycle. Furthermore, some initial field work is likely to occur quite early in the planning stage, as auditors collect information to form the basis for a plan. In addition, the engagement team may find it necessary to engage in ongoing communications with the auditee, first to discuss preliminary findings and then to talk about what will be stated in the auditor's final report.

## Engagement Scope Issues

Defining the scope of an engagement is especially critical to its success, since properly-defined boundaries are needed to ensure that resources are properly targeted. This is a particular concern when a process is very broad and overlaps with other processes. In such cases, one should clearly identify the exact point at which a process begins (with inputs from other processes) and ends (with its outputs becoming inputs to other processes). Several other scope issues that may arise are as follows:

- If the process is repeated in multiple locations, define how many of the locations will be included in the engagement. When a process is essentially being duplicated in multiple locations with standardized procedures, it is generally not efficient to include all locations in the scope of the engagement.
- If some elements of the process were audited recently, it may be possible to exclude them from the current engagement.

Another scope issue is the time period to be covered by the engagement. It may address the state of a process only as of a specific date, or it could cover transactions spanning a longer period of time, such as the preceding quarter or year.

## Understanding the Auditee Issues

As part of the planning process for an engagement, the internal auditor must gain an understanding of the auditee, which typically refers to the specific process that is under review. If this is not done, then the testing plan used by the auditor might not be properly designed for the auditee's specific situation, and so could result in wasted resources because additional tests are needed. The following issues should be examined when engaged in researching the auditee:

- *Analyze process objectives.* The auditor should understand why the process exists. For example, the process might help to meet the auditee's reporting requirements, or assist it in complying with regulations, or assist in meeting its strategic goals.
- *Document operations.* The auditor should have a firm grasp of how the process works. This information can be gained from many sources, including a procedures manual, process maps, narrative descriptions of tasks, and the job descriptions of those involved in the process. This information can be supplemented with interviews that cover such topics as the inputs to and outputs from each task, the activities each person performs, and the types of exceptions or errors found during their work. Also, to determine how effectively these tasks are carried out, one might use analytical procedures and/or computer-assisted data analysis techniques to spot which tasks warrant the use of more detailed testing. Further, the auditor should identify any controls that influence the performance of the process. Finally, one should consider the possibility of fraud occurring within the process, including how this might be accomplished and the potential severity of these acts on the business. The result of this process analysis should be a written description of how the process works, accompanied by a flowchart that depicts the flow of documents and the locations of controls and decision points. The written description should cover the key inputs to and outputs from the process, the key steps in the process, and any risks and controls associated with it.

- *Review risks*. Consider the possibility of events occurring that could negatively impact the achievement of the objectives associated with a process. This can be done with a brainstorming session, as well as by analyzing what has happened to the process in the past, and to similar processes elsewhere in the industry. Then determine the potential likelihood and impact of each risk on the process, to spot which risks could have the greatest negative impact on the process objectives. Those risks with a medium-to-high probability of occurrence and a medium-to-high negative impact on objectives should be addressed in the engagement.
- *Review controls*. Identify all key controls associated with the process. These are any controls whose absence would make it difficult to achieve desired process results. Any control that mitigates a medium or high risk should be classified as a key control. Then link key controls to process-level risks, and decide whether the controls are adequate for mitigating the associated risks, taking into consideration the impact of compensating controls from other processes. Finally, make note of any control gaps in the process, and evaluate the severity of these gaps. The gaps are considered to be preliminary audit observations that should be discussed with management.

## Plan Development Issues

Once information has been collected about the auditee, it is used as input to the development of the engagement plan. This development process is comprised of the following three steps:

- *Develop a test plan*. The test plan should be set up to obtain sufficient appropriate audit evidence to support an evaluation of the effectiveness of operation for key controls. Based on the prior documentation of operations, the auditor can now evaluate which controls are sufficiently important to test. The focus of the testing should be on those controls that were evaluated as having been designed adequately. There is generally no need to test those controls already designated as not having been designed adequately. The testing plan should state the nature of each test to be conducted, the sample size, and the time period that the test is intended to cover.
- *Develop a work program*. The internal audit department may use a standard template for its work program, to ensure that all required tasks are completed. This template typically itemizes the following activities:
  - Administrative activities, such as the scheduling of resources and the establishment of milestone dates.
  - Meetings to address the initial engagement kick-off, as well as subsequent milestone reviews.
  - Task listings, itemizing such activities as understanding the process and identifying key controls.
  - Tests to be conducted.

- o Communication activities, such as drafting the report, discussing it with auditee management, and issuing the final report.
- o Engagement completion steps, such as clearing all review notes and finalizing all working papers.

In cases where the work to be completed is non-standard, it may make sense to construct a more unique template. Whatever the format may be, it should clearly assign responsibility for each task and be updated regularly to reflect the status of each task.

- *Assign resources.* The final step in development of the plan is to estimate the amount of resources needed (mostly auditor time), determine who has the skills needed, and schedule their time onto the engagement project. Outside specialists may need to be brought in for some engagements. Depending on the location of the engagement, it may also call for travel and entertainment expenditures. There may also be technology costs when software licenses are needed for software that will be unique to the engagement.

## Assurance Engagement Communication Issues

The formulation of the communications issued by an internal audit team are based on an analysis of the observations made over the course of the engagement. There are four general categories of reporting required, based on the nature of the observations. In ascending order of importance, these reporting categories are as follows:

1. *Insignificant findings | No key controls.* When the observations result in insignificant findings and do not involve any key controls, one can make informal communications of observations relating to secondary controls. In addition, a formal communication should be made to senior management, noting the absence of observations relating to key controls.
2. *Insignificant findings | Adequate compensating controls.* When the observations result in insignificant findings relating to key controls and there are adequate compensating controls, then a formal communication of these findings should be made to senior management and the outside auditors.
3. *Significant findings.* When the observations are assessed as being significant, then a formal communication of these findings should be sent to senior management, the audit committee, and the outside auditors.
4. *Material findings.* When the observations are assessed as being material, then a formal communication of these findings should be sent to senior management, the audit committee, the outside auditors, and other interested parties as per the applicable financial reporting regulations.

In order to sort observations about controls into the preceding classifications, we need to define the terms insignificant, significant, and material. These classifications should be carefully defined and closely adhered to when evaluating observations, since the outcome can change the type of reporting used. The definitions are as follows:

- *Insignificant deficiency.* When there is a slight chance that a control will fail, or there is a trivial impact when it does fail.
- *Significant deficiency.* When there is a more than remote likelihood that a control will fail, and the impact of its failure is significant.
- *Material deficiency.* When there is a more than remote likelihood that a control will fail, and the impact of its failure exceeds the firm's financial statement materiality threshold.

*Materiality* is the threshold above which missing or incorrect information in financial statements is considered to have an impact on the decision making of users. Materiality is sometimes construed in terms of net impact on reported profits, or the percentage or dollar change in a specific line item in the financial statements. Examples of materiality are as follows:

- A company reports a profit of exactly $10,000, which is the point at which earnings per share exactly meet analyst expectations. Any reduction in profit below this point would have triggered a sell-off of company shares, and so would be considered material.
- A company reports a current ratio of exactly 2:1, which is the amount needed to meet its loan covenants. Any current asset or current liability amounts resulting in a ratio of less than 2:1 would be considered material, since the loan could then be called by the lender.
- A company omits the existence of a lawsuit from its financial statement disclosures that indicates the potential for a large settlement that could bankrupt it.

Based on the preceding examples, it should be clear that sometimes even quite a small change in financial information can be considered material, as well as a simple omission of information.

The internal auditor should issue a stream of communications during an assurance engagement, in order to keep the auditee informed of the team's progress and findings. These communications might take the form of a verbal discussion, a memo, or possibly draft working papers. A high level of communication throughout an engagement increases the quality of the final report, since the audit team will likely receive feedback from the auditee about the reasons for any issues found.

The final document produced by an audit team should state why the engagement was conducted, what it was expected to achieve, the activities and time period covered, and the results of the work. It may also include any responses by the auditee to the conclusions and recommendations of the audit team. Another option is to include background information about the business unit reviewed, the status of any recommendations made in prior engagements, and any improvements since the last audit.

This document must be reviewed and approved by the chief audit executive or some other designated party before it is issued.

> **Tip:** Set a target of issuing the final report within 10 business days of the completion of the closing conference, where the team's preliminary findings are discussed. Doing so keeps the recommendations from becoming stale.

The exact form of the report will depend on its intended audience. If a wide range of recipients is anticipated, then the report will need to include a sufficient discussion of evidence for them to understand the conclusions reached and recommendations for improvement. Conversely, if the report is targeted at a small number of recipients, then it can take the form of a shorter memorandum, stating only the nature of the engagement and providing just enough supporting material to justify the associated conclusions and recommendations.

How to express the overall results of an engagement is up to the audit team, but would likely encompass one of the following three options as they pertain to controls:

- Itemize the observations made about controls, without stating an overall conclusion or expressing any type of assurance about the effectiveness of those controls.
- State that nothing has come up indicating that the auditee's controls are operating in an ineffective manner or are designed inadequately (known as a negative assurance statement).
- State that the auditee's controls are operating effectively and are designed adequately (known as a positive assurance statement).

> **Tip:** Less significant communications may be kept out of the formal final report and instead communicated orally.

Instead of the three preceding options, the department could elect to use a more detailed rating system (possibly involving a numerical value). This system could provide a rating for an overall engagement, or it could individually rate each issue within a report. Doing so gives management and the audit committee a better perspective on audit results across the organization, and can also be used to show results on a trend line.

Ideally, the final report should be issued to anyone in the organization who can ensure that the observations and recommendations made will be given proper consideration. This tends to mean that full reports are given to department managers for action, while summary-level reports are given to senior management, the board of directors, and the audit committee.

> **Note:** The release of some final report information may be restricted if it contains privileged or proprietary information, or is related to illegal acts. These items may be released separately on a need-to-know basis.

**SAMPLE FORMAL REPORT**

**Date:** May 15, 20X1

**To:** Chief Financial Officer

**From:** Internal Audit Manager

**Subject:** Omaha Business Unit Billings Audit Report

The internal audit department completed an internal control review of the Omaha business unit's billings function on May 5, 20X1. The scope of the review was to evaluate the design adequacy and operating effectiveness of the system of internal controls within the billings process. The review included verification procedures to ensure the proper authorization, validity, accuracy, completeness, existence, classification, integrity, and availability of records and other relevant documentation supporting billings processed during the fiscal year ended March 31, 20X0.

The scope of the review included the documentation, evaluation, and testing of the following:

- Procedures for processing shipping documents
- Procedures for preparing customer billings

**Conclusion**

In our opinion, the billings process is reasonable and the system of internal controls is acceptable, resulting in a satisfactory audit rating. This rating indicates that overall internal controls are acceptable to safeguard assets and minimize exposure to loss. The rating also indicates that there are relatively few deficiencies.

**Management's Action Plan**

Management has created a satisfactory action plan to address the observation presented in this report.

Our testing of the billings system confirmed that there is a reasonable process for transferring shipping information from the shipping department to the accounting department, which is then used to create billings. However, we noted that the system is manual, and so depends on the physical transfer of shipping documents between the two departments. We noted delays of as much as three days in making this transfer, which results in similar delays in the issuance of billings.

We recommend that the shipping module interface in the business unit's enterprise resource planning system be activated, so that shipping notifications are sent electronically to the accounting department as soon as shipments occur, thereby eliminating the delay caused by the transfer of documents.

Management has responded that it has given the module interface a high priority in the IT department, and expects that it will be fully tested and implemented within four months.

**Distribution**

Chairman of the Board
Audit Committee
Chief Executive Officer
Chief Financial Officer
Controller
Independent Outside Auditor

## The Assurance Engagement Monitoring Function

Part of the formal report (as noted in the preceding exhibit) should include management's action plan, which management is committing to perform subsequent to the issuance of the report. The internal audit department should have a system in place to monitor how well management follows through on its commitments. The intent is to ensure that corrective actions are taken in a timely manner in order to fix the underlying conditions. If management's actions do not result in the desired reduction in risk, then the situation should be reported at regular intervals (such as quarterly) to senior management and the audit committee.

The time period allowed before the internal audit staff should begin its monitoring activities will be quite short when an observed issue has been classified as material, and can be longer when it was only classified as insignificant. Also, a material observation should trigger quite frequent monitoring follow-ups, until such time as the issue has been remediated.

Monitoring activities should include the use of retesting procedures to ensure that risk mitigation has been achieved. This will only be the case when remediating activities result in controls that are judged to have been designed accurately and which are operating effectively, and when the risk at which it was targeted has been appropriately mitigated.

When management has chosen to accept a risk, rather than mitigating it, the internal audit manager must decide whether that is a prudent choice. If the manager believes that management has accepted an excessively high risk, then he or she should discuss the matter with senior management. If the matter has still not been resolved, then it should be presented to the board. There are no circumstances under which the internal audit manager is responsible for personally resolving the identified risk.

Any monitoring functions undertaken should be documented and stored in the related engagement working papers. This additional documentation can be used as the basis for the next scheduled engagement, part of which is targeted at deciding whether management has fulfilled its action plan commitments.

## The Consulting Engagement

A consulting engagement is not as regimented as the assurance engagements on which the internal audit department spends a large part of its time. Instead, it involves any counseling, advice, training, or facilitation activity on which the engagement customer and the internal audit department can agree. The resulting process is likely to be similar to the one already described for an assurance engagement, though the level of emphasis on the various planning steps may change somewhat, depending on the nature of the engagement.

Consulting engagements tend to be more forward-looking than assurance engagements, which are oriented more toward a business unit's historical results. In many cases, these engagements still relate to the controls that are so frequently targeted by the department's assurance function, since internal auditors are viewed as being experts in the areas of risk management and control systems. However, a consulting engagement is more concerned with setting up new controls for new processes, thereby ensuring that risk levels are minimized and efficiencies are maximized as soon as a process begins to function. Some of the other areas in which the department's expertise can be called upon for consulting engagements are:

- Conduct benchmarking analyses to search for best practices that can be applied to processes.
- Conduct due diligence on target companies that may be acquired, with a particular emphasis on the quality of their control systems.
- Conduct fraud examinations when warnings are received that fraud may be present.
- Conduct reviews of service providers and suppliers.
- Conduct training on the topics of internal control and risk management.
- Facilitate sessions that explore changes in a business unit's risk profile because of changes in the industry or in general economic conditions.
- Facilitate sessions that examine how processes can be improved to better support a business unit's goals.
- Act as an advisor in the development of information systems.
- Review the causes of operational performance issues.
- Deal with special requests from senior management or the board.

In essence, any type of consulting engagement is acceptable, as long as it does not impair the independence of the internal auditors or their objectivity.

Consulting engagements are usually given higher priority when they can be used to mitigate a serious risk or they represent a clear opportunity, such as a major enhancement to the efficiency or effectiveness of a process. They can be prioritized and scheduled most efficiently when they are brought up as part of the annual planning process for the department, so that resources can be reserved for them. However, in some cases consulting engagements arrive with no notice and must be completed quickly, such as fraud investigations and due diligence on acquisition candidates. This means that resources may be unexpectedly drawn away from assurance engagements, which can interfere with the completion of these other engagements. The unexpected nature of these requests can be dealt with to some extent by building excess capacity into the department schedule; doing so gives the internal audit manager enough extra staff to tackle unexpected projects on short notice.

> **Note:** Consulting work is given a higher priority when a business is going through a period of change, since it makes more sense to advise on the structure of new processes than to conduct assurance engagements on processes that are going away.

The planning process for a consulting engagement draws from the process steps used for an assurance engagement, such as gathering evidence, performing analytical procedures, and understanding key risks. In particular, the team members need to have a solid understanding of the engagement objectives and scope, so that they do not waste resources working on areas tangential to the engagement but not actually needed to meet the desired objectives. This may be an iterative process, as the customer needs to be aligned with the engagement team's understanding of the work to be performed, so that it does not have to be cajoled into providing the resources needed to complete the engagement.

Another area of concern is being able to schedule a consulting engagement that is aligned with the scheduling constraints of the people who need to serve on the team. These engagements frequently require the services of people with very particular skill sets, whose time is usually already consumed by other engagements. Consequently, before formally committing to a consulting engagement, one should be absolutely certain that the resources needed will be available within the scheduled time frame. In order to facilitate an engagement, the limited availability of in-house specialists may make it necessary to bring in outside specialists to assist in the engagement.

A final area of concern is to discuss prospective recommendations with the customer, to see if they are practical and require resources that are accessible to the customer. Otherwise, the final report may be full of ineffective advice that is of no use to the customer, and which damages the reputation of the internal audit department.

The communications resulting from consulting engagements are not as structured as those used for assurance engagements. Instead, the final report can vary widely, depending on the scope and purpose of the work to be performed. It may be distributed only to the individual requesting the engagement, or its distribution may be more extensive, depending on the circumstances.

An engagement team should prepare working papers for each consulting engagement, but they do not have to follow the regimented process used in assurance engagements. Instead, the main point is to document the observations found and recommendations made to management, so that the team can adequately back up the reasons for engagement outcomes.

## Summary

The internal audit department's primary work involves assurance engagements, though consulting activities can be quite valuable to the organization. Assurance engagements follow a carefully defined process flow, passing through planning, performance, and communication stages that are useful for ensuring that all required tasks are completed. Of particular concern to the auditor is identifying the boundaries of the project in order to keep from wasting resources, and properly categorizing the resulting observations so that senior management and the board are notified when more critical control issues are found. Consulting engagements tend to be much more free-form, where the audit team can certainly borrow from the process flow used for assurance engagements, but can pare away tasks that are not needed, depending on the nature of the engagement.

# Glossary

## A

*Analytical procedures.* The analysis of comparisons between financial and nonfinancial data, as well as the identification of fluctuations that differ from expectations.

*Application.* A software program that runs on a computer.

*Appropriateness.* The quality of audit evidence collected.

*Attribute sampling.* The selection of a small number of transactions and making assumptions about how their characteristics represent the full population of which the selected items are a part.

*Audit committee.* A subset of a firm's board of directors that is responsible for the oversight of the internal auditors and external auditors.

*Audit evidence.* Any information used by the internal auditor as the basis for his or her conclusions.

*Audit risk.* The risk that an auditor will reach an invalid conclusion.

*Audit sampling.* The use of an audit procedure to select and evaluate less than 100% of a population, where the items selected are expected to be representative of the population, and which can therefore provide a reasonable basis for conclusions about the population.

*Automated control.* A control operated by the computer system through which business transactions are recorded.

## B

*Block sampling.* A sampling approach in which a series of sequential selections are made.

*Business process.* A set of connected tasks that result in the completion of a goal.

*Business process diagram.* A graphical depiction of the flow of a business process.

## C

*Cybersecurity.* The practice of protecting networks, devices, and data from unauthorized access or criminal use, as well as the practice of ensuring confidentiality, integrity, and the availability of information.

## D

*Data analytics.* The science of analyzing raw data in order to reach a conclusion about that data.

*Data center.* A group of networked computer servers that is used for the remote storage, processing, and/or distribution of large amounts of data.

*Data scrubbing.* The removal or modification of data that are incomplete, incorrect, improperly formatted, or duplicated.

*Database.* A data structure that stores organized information.

*Detective control.* A control used to detect control breaches after they have occurred.

*Deviation.* A departure from the expected performance of a targeted control.

**E**

*Embezzlement.* When employees either directly take assets from the company for their own use, or assist in diverting assets from the company.

*Enterprise risk management.* A broad-based system that provides a consistent methodology for locating, measuring, and reporting on risks throughout an organization.

**F**

*False positive.* A test result which incorrectly indicates that a particular condition or attribute is present.

*Firewall.* A barrier between a trusted system or network and outside connections, such as the Internet. It acts as a filter, only allowing trusted data to flow through it.

*Flowchart.* A diagram that graphically describes a business process.

*Fraud.* Any intentional misstatement of the financial statements.

*Fraud triangle.* The three factors that make fraud more likely, which are perceived pressure, opportunity, and rationalization.

**G**

*Governance.* The set of processes employed by the board to oversee how management fulfills the organization's objectives.

**H**

*Haphazard sampling.* A sampling approach that is nonstatistical in nature, but which attempts to approximate a random selection by making selections without any conscious bias.

**I**

*Independence.* The concept that the internal audit function cannot directly engage in company operations, since it would then be working for the management team it is supposed to be evaluating.

*Insignificant deficiency.* When there is a slight chance that a control will fail, or there is a trivial impact when it does fail.

*Internal audit.* The department within a business that monitors the efficacy of its processes and controls.

Glossary

## M

*Manual control.* A control that requires someone to manually perform it.

*Material deficiency.* When there is a more than remote likelihood that a control will fail, and the impact of its failure exceeds the firm's financial statement materiality threshold.

*Materiality.* The threshold above which missing or incorrect information in financial statements is considered to have an impact on the decision making of users.

## N

*Nonsampling risk.* The risk of reaching an erroneous conclusion for any reason other than something related to sampling risk.

*Nonstatistical sampling.* The selection of a test group that is based on the auditor's judgment, rather than a formal statistical method.

*Notable item.* An item spotted within a population that may be indicative of a risk of reaching an incorrect conclusion that had either not been previously assessed or which is higher than originally assessed.

## O

*Objectivity.* Having an unbiased impartial attitude toward one's work, so that no compromises are made in the development of work products.

## P

*Population.* The entire set of data from which a sample is selected, and from which an auditor desires to draw conclusions.

*Preventive control.* A control that keeps a control breach from occurring.

*Project.* A complex series of activities that result in a unique outcome.

## R

*Reasonable assurance.* A high level of assurance regarding whether a company's processes and controls are operating properly.

*Relevance.* The degree to which audit evidence is connected to the purpose of an audit procedure.

*Risk management.* The set of processes used to identify and mitigate any uncertainties that may impact an organization.

## S

*Sampling risk.* The possibility that the items selected in a sample are not truly representative of the population being tested.

*Sampling unit.* Any of the elements that constitute a population.

*Sequential sampling*. The evaluation of each sample taken from a population to see if it fits a desired conclusion.

*Significant deficiency*. When there is a more than remote likelihood that a control will fail, and the impact of its failure is significant.

*Strategic risk*. The probability that an event will interfere with a company's business model.

*Statistical sampling*. The random selection of sample items and the use of probability theory to evaluate sample results.

*Sufficiency*. The quantity of audit evidence collected.

*System of controls*. The policies and procedures used to ensure the integrity of a firm's financial information, promote accountability, and prevent fraud.

*Systematic sampling*. Where a rational technique is used for picking a sample, typically by dividing the number of units in a population by the sample size.

**T**

*Tolerable rate of deviation*. The largest percentage variance experienced in audit sampling that an auditor will accept in order to rely upon a specific control.

**V**

*Vouching*. The process of reviewing documentary evidence to see if it properly supports the item under examination.

**W**

*Working papers*. Documentation of the evidence gathered during an engagement, providing evidence that sufficient information was gathered to support an internal auditor's conclusions.

# Index